Dining in QuartersA

Charleston Naval Base
Charleston, South Carolina

By Donna L. Kaup

GATEWAY PUBLICATIONS, INC.
CHARLESTON, SOUTH CAROLINA

Dining in Quarters A Cookbook

Published by Gateway Publications, Inc.

Library of Congress Catalog Card Number 93-081031
ISBN Number 1-885954-00-X

Designed by Mary Dean Turner Richards

Edited by Kathleen Blanchard

Cover Design and Artwork by E. Jean Smith

Photographs courtesy of
Palmer Olliff
The Charleston Post and Courier
United States Navy

Printed in the United States of America

THIS BOOK IS DEDICATED WITH LOVE

TO MY THREE DAUGHTERS

STACY LEE

JENNIFER JADE

AMY DESIREE

ACKNOWLEDGMENTS

This cookbook has taken over 25 years to compile. I can now toss out all those recipe cards and folders loaded with magazine recipes and newspaper clippings which clutter the kitchen. In particular I want to acknowledge the Honolulu Advertiser, San Diego Tribune, Washington Post, The Charleston Post and Courier, The Seattle Times, Seattle Post-Intelligencer and the book, The Navy in Charleston, for their contributions. Many thanks go to the staff at the Charleston Post and Courier for their help in printing historical photos and to Palmer Olliff for his knowledge and photos of the past of the Charleston Naval Base.

I am grateful to my many relatives and friends for sharing their recipes over these years. The foundation for this cookbook was provided by my family in Seattle who sponsored many potlucks at Lake Cochran, and my mother-in-law in the Missouri Ozarks who shared the secrets of a farmer's wife. I thank my extended family of Navy wives, in particular the submarine wives, whose support, networking, and friendship enriched the lives of our family and made each move enjoyable. To our many friends in Charleston, Washington, DC, San Diego, and Honolulu, I thank you for sharing your recipes with me.

The term "dining-in" is derived from a Viking tradition of celebrating great battles and heroic feats at a formal banquet. This tradition was adopted by our military when the officers' mess was established, and it became known as "dining-in." Because of my Norwegian heritage and my Navy ties, I thought it would be very appropriate to take literary license and entitle my cookbook Dining in Quarters A.

Last, but not least, I especially thank my husband, Karl, for the sea and land adventures all these years, for the opportunity and privilege to meet so many wonderful people, and for his love and encouragment in writing this cookbook; and to our daughters, Stacy, Jennifer, and Amy, who were the true guinea pigs for these recipes.

We truly enjoyed living and DINING IN QUARTERS A on the Charleston Naval Base. This has indeed been the highlight of our time in the Navy.

Donna Kaup
Charleston, 1994

CONTENTS

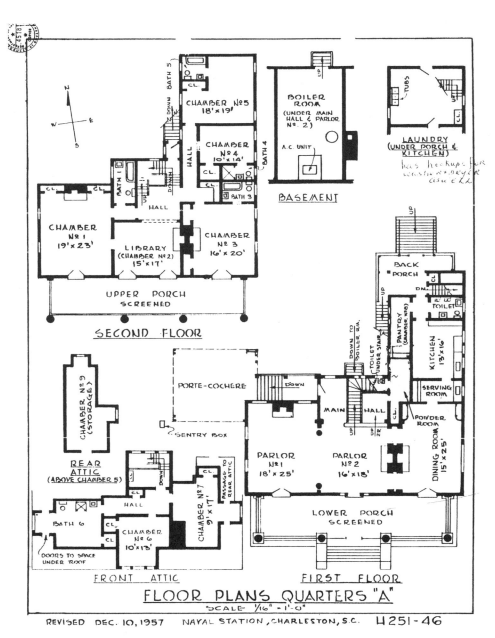

FLOOR PLANS QUARTERS "A"

SCALE 1/16" = 1'-0"

REVISED DEC. 10, 1957   NAVAL STATION, CHARLESTON, S.C.   H 251-46

DINING IN
QUARTERS A

To understand the genesis of Quarters A requires a bird's eye view of this portion of Charleston's Cooper River that would eventually become the Navy Yard, home to this gracious mansion.

In the early 1800's, the rice plantations on the west bank of the Cooper River included Long Point, Marshlands, Retreat, and Oak Grove. This labor intensive crop was a mainstay in the local Charleston economy. After 1865, the rice plantations were no longer cost effective, and the general economy of this area suffered accordingly.

Around 1890, Charleston began to develop Chicora Park on the grounds of the old Turnbull Plantation, previously known as Retreat. The park designer, Olmstead Brothers of Massachusetts, constructed salt water lagoons and landscape gardens, using the experience gained a few years earlier when they designed the magnificent gardens at Biltmore House in Asheville, North Carolina. Now Chicora Park had taken on the look of a first class resort. A wharf was built, along with service buildings, bridges, and a golf course. The 50 year old Turnbull Mansion was renovated into a state-of-the-art inn. A pavilion was built in the park and soon became a gathering place for Charlestonians to picnic and dance on warm summer evenings. A trolley ran from downtown to the entrance of Chicora Park, making it an easy and enjoyable trip.

The Spanish American War in 1898 taxed the Navy's shore facilities. The necessity of maintaining naval stations on each coast to support the fleet in time of crisis became widely known. Shortly after the War, many new navy yards were established.

On 29 June 1900, a board of naval officers, appointed by the Secretary of the Navy, recommended Chicora Park to become a navy yard. Senator Benjamin Ryan Tillman, a powerful member of the Naval Affairs Committee, helped ensure the Navy Yard would be built at Charleston.

Upon selection of the site, approximately 2250 acres of land and marsh areas were purchased at a cost of $110,207.00. The records indicate that at the time the land was purchased, four buildings were located on the site. These buildings were known as the Turnbull Mansion, "Dead House," Gatekeeper's Lodge, and Marshlands Plantation House.

The Turnbull Mansion was located across the road from the future site of Quarters A in the vicinity of Quarters H and I. Shortly after acquisition of the property by the Government, the Turnbull Mansion was destroyed by fire.

The "Dead House", a small brick structure located down the path from the future Quarters A, was built in the 1700's. Because travel was slow in those days, the "Dead House" was used as a cool house where the dead were laid out until relatives and friends arrived for the funeral. The reverse of the Lords Proprietors' Seal is located above the door. As you look at the Seal, you will observe the individual Coats of Arms beginning clockwise in the "noon position": Albemarle, Craven, John Berkeley, Ashley, Carteret, William Berkeley, Colleton, and Clarendon.

The Gatekeeper's Lodge was constructed in 1860. It is located across the road from Quarters A and is in use today as Quarters F, home for the Naval Supply Center Commanding Officer.

The Marshlands House was built by John Ball, a Cooper River rice planter, soon after he bought the plantation here around 1810. After the Navy acquired the property, the house was used for public quarters under the designation of Quarters E until 1953 when it was redesignated "Building 16" and assigned to non-residential use by Shipyard Watch and Duty Officers. In clearing the site for Dry Dock No. 5, "Building 16" was donated to the City of Charleston and subsequently floated down the Cooper River to Fort Johnson on James Island where it is presently the office of the South Carolina Wildlife and Marine Resource Department. The U.S. Fish and Wildlife Service offices are located in the basement. Many years ago photographs were taken of the moldings and fireplaces of the Marshlands House to help in the renovations of the White House since both great houses were built in the early 1800's.

Quarters A was one of the first construction projects after the Navy established the yard. Under an act of 1 July 1902, $12,000 was appropriated for the construction of quarters for the Commandant of the Charleston Navy Yard. Contract number 1143 dated 30 September 1904 was awarded to Isaac W. Nailor of Milton, Delaware, for construction of Quarters A. The cost was $10,999.00. Construction of the quarters commenced in 1904 and was

DINING IN QUARTERS A

completed in 1905. The 5218 square foot home, not including porches, utility rooms, and storage areas, stands today as it was built, with only the addition of the porte-cochere in 1936 and a rear porch extension in 1944. The front patio was constructed during World War II. Included in the otherwise random pattern of the red tile chips is a cross oriented "North" and the numbers 1943 denoting the year of construction.

In the early days, six fireplaces gave warmth to the rooms. Over the years, plumbing and heating facilities have been upgraded and air conditioning added to increase the habitability of the 12-room house.

The lower floor features a spacious dining room and two parlors. Four large bedrooms, four baths, and a library comprise the second floor. On the third floor are the old "servants" living quarters with a bath, sitting room, bedroom, and a secret passageway and hidden room that once may have served as quarters for the chambermaid.

Quarters A features a spacious dining room.

The original furnishings of the house, some of which remain today, were derived from a standard allowance of furniture compiled by the Navy Bureau of Yards and Docks in Washington, DC. Authorization was given to outfit the new quarters with Brussels carpet, not to exceed a cost of $1.15 a yard, a sofa not to exceed $50, and several chairs at a cost of $12.50 and $25 each. The bedroom plan called for brass or iron bedsteads, a bureau with mirrors, washstand, chairs, rocker, and carpet, all not to exceed a total of $100.

Quarters A exemplifies the best of southern living. While the Charleston Naval Base has grown and changed complexion over the years, Quarters A — with its four tall white columns, towering oaks, and sweeping views of the Cooper River and marshlands beyond — has retained the graciousness and charm that is so much a part of the Lowcountry.

An aerial view of The Navy Yard around 1930. A ship is entering the dry dock in the center of the picture. USS Hartford is moored by the quay wall at the lower right of the picture.

HISTORY OF THE CHARLESTON NAVAL BASE

The 56th Congress of the United States passed an act in 1900 authorizing the Secretary of the Navy to investigate a proposed move of the Port Royal Naval Station, near Beaufort, SC, to a site near the city of Charleston, SC. Then Secretary of the Navy, John D. Long, appointed a board of naval officers to conduct an investigation of the proposal. The board's recommendation was to have a Navy Yard established on the west bank of the Cooper River, approximately six miles north of the Customs House in the City of Charleston. A site encompassing three antebellum plantations was selected and purchased in July 1901, with additional land purchases made later.

The first naval officer was assigned duty in early 1902. A work force was organized, the Yard was surveyed, and construction of buildings and a dry dock began. The dry dock was finished in 1909, and red brick buildings and the main power plant, still in use today, were completed about the same time.

With a work force of some 300 civilians, the first ship was placed in the dry dock and work began on vessels of the fleet in 1910. Improvement of facilities and a gradual increase in the work force took place during succeeding years, and in 1915 there were approximately 800 civilians employed at the Yard.

The Sixth Naval District, which originally included only the states of South Carolina and Georgia, received its first recognition as a separate entity in 1916 when the commandant was instructed to establish separate files for the district and the Navy Yard. In May 1917, separate offices for the district were established in downtown Charleston. By the end of World War I, 93 officers were attached to district headquarters.

During World War I, a Naval Training Center was established. At the same time there was expansion of facilities, land area, and the work force of the Navy Yard, with employment reaching 6,500 personnel in November 1918. The Yard built two gunboats, several subchasers and tugs in addition to repairs and other services to the fleet. Following the war, the work force was gradually reduced, and only minor vessels were sent to Charleston for repairs. With an employment level of 500 workers and only an occasional minesweeper or seagoing tug to repair, the status of the Navy Yard was uncertain from 1922 to 1933.

Following the war, in 1919, the district headquarters was moved back to the Navy Yard, the district commandant position and training center were disestablished, and the Navy Yard commandant was given additional duties as district commandant. The district area of responsibility grew to include South Carolina, Georgia, most of North Carolina and Florida, plus the states of Alabama, Tennessee, Mississippi, Louisiana, and Texas.

District activities soon were over-shadowed by Charleston Navy Yard activities, however. The year 1933 marked the beginning of an upsurge at the Yard. A larger workload, principally in construction of several Coast Guard tugs, a Coast Guard cutter, and a Navy gunboat, created the need for more facilities and a much larger work force. This force formed the nucleus of the large group of men and women required to meet the demands of naval shipbuilding and repair work during World War II. The war brought further expansion of Yard facilities and the acquisition of large land areas known as the "South Yard," "Naval Air Station," and the "Noisette Creek Area."

During World War II, Navy Yard employees constructed some 200 vessels of various classes including destroyers, destroyer escorts, tank landing ships, amphibious landing ships, and destroyer tenders. In addition, there was a great amount of battle damage and repair work conducted during the period. Civilian employment at the yard peaked in 1943 with almost 26,000

The James E. Craig (DE-201) and the Eichenberger (DE-202) are ready for launching.

employees working three shifts daily.

Meanwhile, the Sixth Naval District was responsible for the protection of sea lanes and convoy routes off the coast of the district, a total coastline of about 540 miles. April 1943 set the record for reported submarine contacts in coastal waters of the district, with 35 hostile contacts investigated. The busiest area for anti-submarine patrols was right off the coast of Charleston. Other areas of intensive anti-submarine efforts were off Jacksonville and Fernandina, Florida, and Cape Fear, Savannah and St. Simons Island, Georgia. As a result, only three U.S. ships were torpedoed off the Carolinas and Georgia coasts after May 1942.

The most publicized war incident in the Sixth Naval District area occurred on 9 May 1942, when a German submarine was sunk by the Coast Guard Cutter *Icarus*. *Icarus* was off the North Carolina coast when a German U-boat fired a torpedo at the cutter. The weapon missed and exploded about 200 feet astern. *Icarus* began attacking with depth charges. After the eleventh depth charge exploded, the damaged submarine surfaced for a short time, and 33 members of its crew, including the captain, abandoned ship. *The Icarus* rescued the German sailors and brought them to Charleston. Other crew members were lost when the submarine sank.

German submarine crew members at the Charleston Naval Base, May 1942.

Just prior to the outbreak of World War II, on 5 November 1941, the Naval Base complex had been enlarged with the establishment of the Charleston Naval Ammunition Depot. Located approximately 20 miles from downtown Charleston on the west bank of the Cooper River, the site initially encompassed five plantations in the Goose Creek area of St. James Parish. During World War II, the depot was actively engaged in receiving, storing, reworking, and issuing ammunition.

From 1903 to 1945, except for a short period during World War I, the commandant of the Charleston Navy Yard also served as commandant of the Sixth Naval District. This dual command relationship ceased on 30 November 1945, when the U.S. Naval Base Charleston was established. At the same time, the Navy Yard became the Charleston Naval Shipyard, a component of the Naval Base, with a separate commander. The district commandant was given additional duty as commander of the Charleston Naval Base.

The Sixth Naval District was enlarged on 1 September 1948, when it absorbed the Seventh Naval District, including all of the state of Florida, plus three states formerly within the Eighth Naval District — Alabama, Mississippi, and Tennessee. This expansion gave the Sixth Naval District the seven states of the southeastern section of the United States and the longest coastline of any district in the country, 2,936 miles.

The ammunition depot was placed in "partial maintenance" status in February 1950. During the Korean War the status of the depot was changed to "maintenance," and to active status in April 1952. In January 1954, an additional tract of land on five other plantations known as the Liberty Hall Annex was acquired from the U.S. Army for future expansion of the depot. The Marine Barracks, Charleston, was established under the commanding officer at the depot in March 1959. Prior to that date, the Marines had been assigned to Marine Barracks, Naval Base, Charleston.

During the 1950s, the Naval Shipyard became the major overhaul facility on the East Coast for submarines, as well as the outfitter for new ships constructed for the Navy in private shipyards in the district.

In 1959, the construction began on new piers, barracks, and buildings for mine warfare ships and personnel. Charleston became a major home port for combatant ships and submarines of the U.S. Atlantic Fleet. Related operational staffs and fleet support commands also arrived in Charleston.

On 1 October 1979, naval districts were disestablished. However, the Charleston Naval Base commander retained Atlantic Fleet regional coordination responsibilities for South Carolina and most of Georgia, as well as some Chief of Naval Operations area coordination responsibilities for naval shore activities and personnel in the former Sixth Naval District.

HISTORY OF THE CHARLESTON NAVAL BASE

The Naval Ammunition Depot was renamed the Naval Weapons Station on 1 September 1965. In 1990 it covered 16,344 acres, which included the 927 acre site of the former Charleston Army Depot acquired by the Navy in 1980. Also in 1980, the Naval Station grew by 42.5 acres with the addition of a former Air Force radar squadron site near the Charleston International Airport.

In 1993, during the third round of the Base Realignment and Closure (BRAC) actions, the commission, headed by James Courter, voted to close the Naval Shipyard and the Naval Station.

This event was greeted with disbelief and disappointment by the Charleston community. However, the necessity for such drastic action was understood in light of our having won the Cold War.

The same expertise, courage, and foresight that made Charleston a world class Navy community was immediately applied to plan for the redevelopment and reuse of this base. Undoubtedly, this property with its miles of deep waterfront, the numerous industrial facilities, and the charming residential area will once again be a centerpiece for the trident region's economic development. Perhaps Chicora Park can be rebuilt, and again residents may take a trolley to the Gatekeeper's cottage below Quarters A to spend a peaceful afternoon on the banks of the Cooper River.

Gatekeeper's Cottage

11

RADM E. S. PRIME	MAY	1905
CAPT S. W. VERY	SEP	1905
CAPT G. L. DYER	APR	1906
RADM J. D. ADAMS	JAN	1909
RADM C. E. FOX	JUN	1910
RADM J. M. HELM	OCT	1911
RADM J. R. EDWARDS	OCT	1914
RADM B. C. BRYAN	JUL	1915
RADM F. E. BEATTY	AUG	1919
RADM E. A. ANDERSON	NOV	1919
RADM A. P. NIBLACK	JUL	1922
RADM G. W. WILLIAMS	AUG	1923
CAPT M. E. TRENCH	SEP	1924
CAPT F. A. TRAUT	SEP	1925
RADM N. A. McCULLY	SEP	1927
RADM J. J. RABY	SEP	1927
RADM E. B. FENNER	MAY	1934
RADM H. V. BUTLER	JUL	1936
RADM W. H. ALLEN	MAR	1938
RADM W. A. GLASSFORD	JUN	1942
RADM JULES JAMES	MAY	1943
RADM L. T. DUBOSE	NOV	1945
RADM R. W. HAYLER	MAY	1948
RADM G. B. DAVIS	JUL	1951

COMMANDANTS, SIXTH NAVAL DISTRICT

RADM H. N. McLEAN	JUL	1953
RADM G. C. CRAWFORD	NOV	1954
RADM J. C. DANIELS	FEB	1958
RADM K. M. McMANES	SEP	1959
RADM L. R. DASPIT	AUG	1962

OCCUPANTS OF QUARTERS A

RADM J. S. DORSEY	JUL	1965
RADM H. J. KOSSLER	JUL	1968
RADM GRAHAM TAHLER	MAY	1973
RADM J. T. BURKE, JR.	DEC	1974
RADM R. F. HOFFMAN	JUL	1976
RADM R. B. McCLINTON	OCT	1979

COMMANDERS, NAVAL BASE CHARLESTON

RADM R. B. McCLINTON	OCT	1980
COMO D. W. COCKFIELD	SEP	1982
COMO D. G. PRIMEAU	OCT	1984
RADM D. G. PRIMEAU	NOV	1985
RADM D. W. COCKFIELD	AUG	1986
RADM W. N. JOHNSON	FEB	1987
RADM W. W. MATHIS	MAY	1989
RADM S. E. BUMP	AUG	1989
RADM K. L. KAUP	NOV	1991
RADM T. J. ROBERTSON	OCT	1993

"THEY THAT GO DOWN TO THE SEA IN SHIPS,
THAT DO BUSINESS IN GREAT WATERS,
THESE SEE THE WORKS OF THE LORD,
AND HIS WONDERS IN THE DEEP."

Psalm 107:23, 24

notes

Beverages

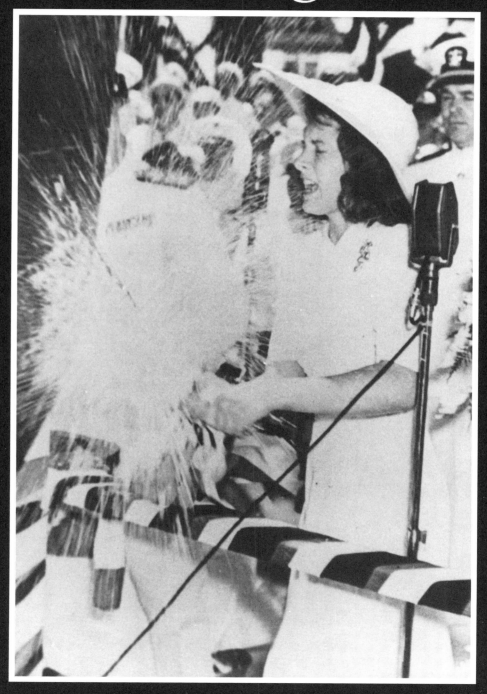

Beverages

Bourbon Slush

Bridal Shower and Christening Punch

Coffee Punch

Coffee Punch served at Quarters A "Open House"

Happy Drink

Holiday Punch

Hot Buttered Rum

Hot Cider Punch

Orange Freeze

Orange Julius

Russian Tea

Summertime Iced Tea

Photo page 15
In July of 1941, Jean Corry christens the Corry (DD-463) before it slides down the ways. On D-day, 6 June 1944, the destroyer struck a mine in the English Channel and sank. Many of her survivors were picked up by the Hobson (DD-464), her Charleston-built sister ship.

Bourbon Slush

2   tea bags

1   cup boiling water

1   cup sugar

3¹/₂ cups water

1   (6 oz.) can frozen orange juice
     concentrate, thawed

¹/₂ cup bourbon

¹/₂ (6 oz.) can frozen lemonade
    concentrate, thawed

Steep tea bags in the 1 cup boiling water 2-3 minutes. Remove tea bags. Stir in sugar. Add remaining ingredients; mix till sugar is dissolved. Pour into freezer containers; freeze firm. Remove from freezer about 10 minutes before serving. Spoon into cocktail glasses; garnish with melon wedges, if desired. Keep unused portion in freezer. Yield: 1¹/₂ quarts.

Bridal Shower and Christening Punch
"Charleston Style"

2   (12 oz.) cans frozen orange juice

2   (12 oz.) cans frozen lemonade (not pink)

2   large cans pineapple juice

1   cup Lipton tea (3 tea bags in one cup of hot water — steep 5 minutes)

1   quart ginger ale

3   large packages frozen strawberries — optional

Pour all ingredients in punch bowl that has an ice ring in it (frozen block of ice). You can also freeze some strawberries in a Jello mold filled with water to use as an ice ring. Yield: 40 punch cup servings.

Coffee Punch

1 **quart strong coffee**
¹/₂ **cup sugar**
1 **pint whipping cream, whipped**
1 **pint vanilla ice cream**

Cool coffee in refrigerator overnight. Next day, cut ice cream and whipped cream into coffee in punch bowl, stirring a little. Yield: 2 quarts.

Coffee Punch served at Quarters A "Open House"

1 **gallon coffee ice cream**
1 **gallon strong coffee (cold)**
1 **gallon milk**

3 **T. almond extract**
1 **can Hershey's syrup (large)**

Mix well in large punch bowl. Yield: 48 cups.

Happy Drink

1 **(12 oz.) frozen concentrate orange juice**
1 **(12 oz.) frozen concentrate lemonade**
3 **cups water**

Combine and pour into a freezer container. Freeze. Mix 1 cup of the frozen slush with **1 cup water** and **1 jigger rum**. Yield: 6 servings.

Holiday Punch

1   **(46 oz.) Hawaiian Punch**
1   **(46 oz.) pineapple juice**
1   **(12 oz.) can frozen orange juice**
4   **cups sparkling cider or ginger ale**

Mix ingredients together in large punch bowl. Float orange slices or strawberries on top or add scoops of raspberry sherbet. Yield: 34 servings of $1/2$ cup each.

Hot Buttered Rum

1 **lb. butter, softened**	1 **quart vanilla ice cream, softened**
1 **lb. box light brown sugar**	**light rum**
1 **lb. box powdered sugar**	**whipped cream**
2 **t. cinnamon**	**cinnamon sticks**
2 **t. nutmeg**	

Combine butter, sugar, and spices; beat until light and fluffy. Add ice cream, and stir until well blended. Spoon mixture into a 2 quart freezer-proof container; freeze. To serve, thaw slightly. Place 3 T. butter mixture and 1 jigger of rum in a large mug; fill with boiling water, stirring well. (Any unused butter mixture can be refrozen.) Top with whipped cream, and serve with a cinnamon stick. Yield: 25 cups.

Hot Cider Punch

1 **quart cranberry juice**	2 **whole cloves**
2 **quarts apple cider**	4 **cinnamon sticks**
$2/3$ **cup brown sugar**	

Heat the combined ingredients slowly over low heat. Serve on a cool autumn evening with friends. Yield: 12 cups.

Orange Freeze

2	pints orange sherbet
4	eggs

2	large oranges,
	peeled and seeded

Whirl in a blender until smooth. Pour into 6 (frosted from freezer) glasses and garnish with orange wedges. Yield: 6 servings.

Orange Julius

1	(6 oz.) can frozen orange
	concentrate
1	cup milk
1	cup water

1/2	cup sugar
1	t. vanilla
6-8	ice cubes

Mix together in a blender. Yield: 4 servings.

Russian Tea

2	cups Tang
2	cups sugar
2/3	t. cloves
2/3	t. cinnamon

1	cup instant tea
2	pkgs. (small) Wylers instant
	lemonade mix

Mix together. Add 3 teaspoons to 1 cup boiling water per serving. Yield: 3 1/2 cups.

Summertime Iced Tea

**Steep 6 tea bags in 4 cups boiling water for 5 minutes.
Add:**

1 1/2	cups sugar
1	(6 oz.) frozen orange or limeade

1	(6 oz.) can frozen lemonade
10	cups water

Combine and chill. Yield: 1 gallon.

Appetizers

The first dry-docking at the Navy Yard was 7 April 1909. The vessel is the naval tug Potomac.

Appetizers

Artichoke Dip

Cheese-Filled Phyllo Triangles

Cheese Puffs

Chicken Liver Pate

Chutney Roll

Clam Appetizer Dip

Dill Weed Dip • Ham Roll-ups

Hot Crab Dip

Jezebel Sauce

Key West Raw Oysters

Makisushi

Marinated Chicken Wings

Mexican Nacho Dip • Mushroom Logs

Pesto and Cheese Appetizer

Pesto Cheese Mold

Pickapeppa Appetizer

Quick Pita Toasts

Round Bread Dip

Spinach Dip • Spinach Squares

Stuffed Snow Peas

Sushi Rice

Artichoke Dip

2   cans (14 oz. each)   1   cup mayonnaise
    artichoke hearts, drained   1   cup sour cream
2   cups freshly grated   1   t. Tabasco sauce
    Parmesan cheese

In food processor, chop artichokes. Add remaining ingredients.

Pour into a 4 cup baking dish and bake 25 minutes at 300°. Serve warm with corn chips or small slices of French bread. Yield: 6-8 servings.

Cheese-Filled Phyllo Triangles

$^1/_3$ cup feta cheese, crumbled
$^1/_3$ cup cream-styled cottage cheese
1   egg, slightly beaten
      dash of salt
      dash of pepper
      dash of ground nutmeg
7   sheets commercial frozen phyllo pastry, thawed
$^2/_3$ cup butter, melted

Combine feta cheese and cottage cheese. Add egg and seasonings, beating well; set aside.

Cut sheets of phyllo lengthwise into 2 inch strips; keep covered with a damp towel until used. Brush 1 strip of phyllo with melted butter. Place 1 teaspoon cheese mixture at base of phyllo strip; fold the right bottom corner over it into a triangle. Continue folding back and forth into a triangle to end of strip. Repeat process with remaining phyllo and cheese mixture.

Place triangles, seam side down, on greased cookie sheets; brush tops with melted butter. Bake at 350° for 20 minutes. Freeze between layers of waxed paper. To cook when frozen: bake hard from freezer at 350° for about 15 minutes. Yield: 3$^1/_2$ dozen.

23

Cheese Puffs

1	loaf unsliced bread	2	egg whites
¹/₂	cup butter	¹/₄	lb. sharp cheese
1	(3 oz.) pkg. cream cheese		

Melt the cheese and butter in a double boiler. Beat the egg whites until stiff.

Cut bread into 1 inch cubes. Fold the egg whites into cheese and dip the bread cubes into mixture until they are covered. Chill on a cookie sheet. Bake at 400° about 20 minutes or until golden brown. Yield: 8-10 servings.

Chicken Liver Pate

1	lb. chicken livers	¹/₄	t. nutmeg
1	onion, chopped	1¹/₂	t. dry mustard
¹/₂	t. pepper	4	t. brandy
¹/₄	t. mace	³/₄	cup butter, melted

Cook chicken livers in small amount of water until tender. Drain. In a food processor mix all ingredients. Salt to taste. Pack in mold and refrigerate. Serve on Melba toast or party rye bread. Yield: 6-8 servings.

Chutney Roll

1 (8 oz.) pkg. cream cheese, softened
¹/₂ cup chutney, finely chopped
¹/₂ cup chopped almonds, toasted
1 T. curry powder
¹/₂ t. dry mustard
¹/₂ cup finely chopped unsalted peanuts

Combine first 5 ingredients in a mixing bowl; stir well. Shape into a log; wrap in waxed paper, and chill 1 hour. Mixture will be soft. Roll log in peanuts. Chill several hours or overnight. Serve with crackers. Yield: 4-6 servings.

Clam Appetizer Dip

1	(8 oz.) pkg. cream cheese	2	t. lemon juice
$^1/_2$	cup sour cream	2	t. Worcestershire sauce
2	T. minced onion	1	can minced clams, drained
1	T. parsley		

Beat the cream cheese till smooth. Beat in sour cream. Stir in remaining ingredients. Cover and chill at least one hour. Serve with chips or crackers. Yield: 4-6 servings.

Dill Weed Dip

$^2/_3$	cup mayonnaise	1	t. Beau Monde Seasoning
$^2/_3$	cup sour cream	1	t. dill weed
1	T. parsley flakes		

Mix all ingredients together. Great for vegetable dip. Yield: $1^1/_2$ cups.

Ham Roll-Ups

1	(3 oz.) pkg. cream cheese	$^1/_2$	t. prepared mustard
$^1/_2$	cup shredded Cheddar cheese	4	slices Oscar Mayer ham
1	t. chopped green onion		(thinly sliced, fully-cooked)

Soften cream cheese; stir in Cheddar cheese, green onion, and mustard. Spread cheese mixture on ham slices. Roll ham from narrow end. Cut each roll into 4 pieces. Secure with wooden pick. Yield: 2-4 servings.

Hot Crab Dip

2	(8 oz.) pkg. cream cheese, room temperature
4	t. creamed horseradish
2	T. onion, finely chopped
2	T. milk
4	t. Worcestershire sauce
1/2	t. salt
	dash of pepper
16	oz. fresh crab meat
	sliced or slivered almonds

Mix cream cheese with milk. Mix together with rest of ingredients. Put in quiche dish. Sprinkle almonds on top. Bake at 350° for 20-30 minutes until bubbly. Serve with crackers or small bread. Yield: 4 cups.

Jezebel Sauce

1	small can dry mustard	1	(10 oz.) jar apple jelly
1	small jar horseradish	1	T. coarsely ground black pepper
1	(10 oz.) jar apricot preserves		

Combine and refrigerate indefinitely. Pour 1/2 cup over **8 oz. package of cream cheese** and serve with crackers. Yield: 3 cups.

Key West Raw Oysters

Wash and clean oysters. Open **raw oysters** and free from the shell.

Top each oyster with **1 t. sour cream**. Top the sour cream with 1/4 **t. caviar** (either red or black).

To serve, place the raw oyster in the shell on a bed of shredded lettuce. Serve 2 oysters per plate.

Makisushi

bamboo rolling mat, available in Japanese stores
sushi rice (page 32)
nori seaweed, Japanese section at the market
wasabi, Japanese horseradish

Place a sheet of nori seaweed, shiny side down, on the bamboo mat. The mat should lie so it rolls away from you, not from side to side.

Keeping your hands moistened with vinegar water, put about $1/2$ cup of sushi rice in the center of the nori and spread evenly over $2/3$ of the nori to a thickness of about $1/2$ inch. Leave about one inch margin at the top of the nori to seal the roll. Spread a streak of washabi across the middle of the rice.

To roll, fold the bamboo mat so that it touches the rice, lift the mat and finish rolling. Roll again with the mat and apply slight pressure to tighten the roll. The most difficult part of making makisushi is getting the roll tight enough to prevent it from disintegrating when it is sliced.

Place the roll on a cutting board, seam side down. Slice the roll into desired thickness—usually 1 inch, using a wet, sharp knife. Cut firmly, straight down. Turn the slices rice side up for decorative effect. Yield: 4-6 slices each roll.

Marinated Chicken Wings

3	lb. chicken wings	$1/2$	cup butter (not margarine)
1	cup soy sauce	1	t. dry mustard
1	cup brown sugar	$1/2$	cup water

Disjoint chicken wings; discard tips. Mix remaining ingredients; heat thoroughly. Add chicken; marinate for at least 2 hours. Place chicken and marinade in baking pan. Bake at 350° for 45 minutes. Remove chicken from marinade; drain on cake racks. To serve at a later date, place in foil; seal. Freeze. Place foil-wrapped chicken in baking pan. Bake at 350° for 1 hour. Serve hot. Yield: 6-8 servings.

Mexican Nacho Dip

2   cans bean dip or one large can refried beans

1   (8 oz.) container avocado dip or use 2-3 ripe avocados
mashed with dash of lemon juice to retain color

2   cups sour cream

1   (8 oz.) jar hot taco sauce

2   ripe tomatoes, chopped and drained on paper towel

1   large green pepper, finely chopped

1/2 cup sliced black olives, drained

1   (8 oz.) Monterey Jack cheese, grated

In a 9 x 13 inch glass dish, layer ingredients in order and chill at least 4 hours or overnight. Serve with Doritos. Yield: 8-10 servings.

Mushroom Logs

2   (8 oz.) cans refrigerated crescent dinner rolls

1   (8 oz.) pkg. cream cheese, softened

1   (4 oz.) can mushroom stems and pieces, drained and chopped

1   t. salt

1   egg, beaten

1-2 T. poppy seeds

Separate crescent dough into 8 rectangles; press perforations to seal.

Combine cream cheese, mushrooms, and salt, mixing well. Spread mushroom mixture in equal portions over each rectangle of dough. Starting at long sides, roll up each rectangle jellyroll fashion; pinch seams to seal. Slice logs into 1 inch pieces; place seam side down on an ungreased baking sheet.

Brush each log with beaten egg, and sprinkle with poppy seeds. Bake in 375° oven for 10-12 minutes. Yield: 4 dozen.

Pesto and Cheese Appetizer

1	cup firmly packed fresh basil	1/3	cup olive oil	
1/2	cup firmly packed fresh parsley	1	(8 oz.) pkg. cream cheese	
2	cloves garlic	1/2	cup whipping cream	
3/4	cup Parmesan cheese, grated	1	(8 oz.) Brie, rind removed	
1/4	cup pinenuts			

In food processor combine basil, parsley, garlic, Parmesan cheese, and pinenuts. Gradually add oil with processor running until consistency of soft butter. Bring cream cheese and Brie to room temperature and beat together until smooth. Beat whipping cream to soft peaks; fold into cheeses. Line a 4-cup mold with plastic wrap. Spread one-fourth of cheese mixture in mold; add one-third of pesto and repeat layers, ending with cheese. Cover and chill for several hours or overnight. Invert mold onto serving plate; garnish with fresh basil. Serve with crackers or thinly-sliced French bread. Yield: 8-10 servings.

Pesto Cheese Mold

1	(16 oz.) pkg. cream cheese, softened at room temperature
1/2	lb. unsalted butter, softened at room temperature
1/2	cup pesto sauce (page 157)

Beat the cream cheese with the butter with an electric mixer until light and fluffy.

Line a 1 quart bowl with a sheet of plastic wrap. Place 1/4 of the cheese mixture in the bottom, smoothing it into an even layer. Top with 1/3 of the pesto, and then repeat with the layers of cheese and pesto, ending with a layer of cheese. Refrigerate until firm, at least three hours, or overnight. To serve, invert the bowl into a platter, and peel off the plastic wrap. Serve with crackers or small pieces of French bread.

The mold can be made up a week in advance and refrigerated, tightly covered with plastic wrap. Unmold just before serving. Yield: 3 1/2 cups.

Pickapeppa Appetizer

1   small bottle Pickapeppa sauce   **1   (8 oz.) pkg. cream cheese**

Place the cream cheese on a wooden plate. Pour enough Pickapeppa over the top of the cream cheese to cover and serve with crackers. Yield: 4-6 servings.

Quick Pita Toasts

pita bread   **garlic powder**
butter or margarine, softened   **Parmesan cheese**

Separate pita bread into two circles; cut each circle in quarters. Spread each with butter and sprinkle with garlic powder to taste and Parmesan cheese. Bake 5 to 10 minutes on cookie sheet at 350° until cheese bubbles and bread begins to brown around edges. Good, quick bread to serve with salads and soups.

Round Bread Dip

1   loaf round bread, rye,   **2   t. chopped onion**
**   pumpernickel, or sourdough**   **2   t. chopped parsley**
2   packages of corned beef,   **2   t. chopped chives**
**   chopped**   **1   t. dill weed**
¹/₂ cup sour cream   **1   t. garlic powder**
¹/₂ cup mayonnaise   **1   t. Beau Monde seasoning**

Mix all ingredients except the bread. Scoop out bread and fill with dip. Use scooped-out pieces for dipping, along with crackers. As dip disappears, use knife to cut bread and dip into cavity. Yield: 1¹/₂ cups.

Spinach Dip

1 pkg. Knorr vegetable soup mix	6 green onions, chopped
1 cup mayonnaise	1 pkg. (10 oz.) chopped spinach,
1 cup sour cream	cooked and drained well
1 cup water chestnuts, minced	1 round caraway rye bread

Mix all ingredients except bread. Hollow out the caraway rye bread and pour the mixture into it and serve with rye crackers. Yield: 4 cups.

Spinach Squares

1 cup flour	6 T. butter, softened
1 t. salt	1 (10 oz.) pkg. frozen spinach
1 t. baking powder	or 2 cups fresh
2 eggs, beaten	1 lb. sharp Cheddar cheese, grated
1 cup milk	1 onion, chopped

Sift flour, salt, and baking powder into a large bowl. Add eggs, milk, and butter and mix well. If using fresh spinach: cook, drain, and chop. If using frozen spinach: cook and drain. Add spinach, cheese, and onion to flour and egg mixture. Spread into a greased 9 x 13 inch pan and bake at 350° for 30 minutes. Cool 10-15 minutes or long enough to cut into squares. Serve warm. Yield: 10-12 servings.

Stuffed Snow Peas

1 clove garlic, minced	1 t. lemon juice
1/4 cup parsley, chopped	1/4 cup dill, chopped
1 (8 oz.) pkg. cream cheese, softened	snow peas, split

Blend ingredients and chill. Stuff into split snow peas on curved side letting some filling show. Yield: 8-10 servings.

Sushi Rice

To make good sushi, the rice must be cooked in the right way.

3   cups Calrose rice

4   cups water

Vinegar Mixture:

¹/₃   cup sushi vinegar

5   T. sugar

1   T. salt

Wash rice until the wash water runs clean and drain in colander.

Place rice in a rice cooker or in a pot with close-fitting lid and add water. Bring rice to a boil and continue to boil until water level is at the rice level. Cover and remove from heat. Let stand for 20 minutes.

While rice is cooking, combine the vinegar mixture in a pan and heat slowly till the sugar has dissolved, stirring constantly. Remove from heat. To cool quickly, place the pan in a bowl of ice cubes.

Empty rice into a nonmetallic tub or wooden bowl and spread it evenly over the bottom with a large wooden spoon. Do not use anything metal, as it may react with the vinegar and create a bad taste. Run the spoon through the rice in right-and-left slicing motions to separate the grains. As you do this, slowly add the vinegar mixture. Avoid adding too much. You do not want mushy rice.

The rice will eventually take on a glossy appearance. This is the end result. Sushi rice can be kept for several hours at room temperature, covered with a damp cloth. Do not refrigerate. Yield 6 cups.

Use sushi rice to make makisushi (page 27).

Soups & Stews

Feeding huge numbers of Navy Yard workers was a massive undertaking in August of 1944.

Soups and Stews

Baked Potato Soup

Black Bean Soup

Cheese-Pumpkin Soup

Clam Chowder

Cream of Broccoli Soup

Cream of Garlic Soup

Elegant Mushroom Soup

French Market Soup

French Onion Soup

Gazpacho

Honolulu Academy Chicken Curry Soup

Hot and Spicy Chicken Soup

Minestrone

Pumpkin Soup

Savory Grouper Stew

She-Crab Soup

Strawberry Soup

Tomato-Ginger Soup

Tortilla Soup

Vichyssoise

Baked Potato Soup

   4   **large baking potatoes**
  $^2/_3$ **cup butter or margarine**
  $^2/_3$ **cup all-purpose flour**
   6   **cups milk**
  $^3/_4$ **t. salt**
  $^1/_2$ **t. pepper**
   4   **green onions, chopped and divided**
  12   **slices bacon, cooked, crumbled, and divided**
  $1^1/_2$ **cups shredded Cheddar cheese, divided**
   1   **(8 oz.) carton sour cream**

Wash potatoes and prick several times with a fork. Bake in a 400° oven for 1 hour or until done. Let cool. Cut potatoes in half lengthwise; scoop out pulp and set aside. Discard skins.

Melt butter in a heavy saucepan over low heat. Add flour, stirring until smooth. Cook one minute, stirring constantly. Gradually add milk. Cook over medium heat, stirring constantly until mixture is thick and bubbly. Add potato pulp, salt, pepper, 2 T. green onions, $^1/_2$ cup bacon, and 1 cup cheese. Cook until thoroughly heated. Stir in sour cream. Add extra milk, if necessary, for desired consistency. Serve with remaining onions, bacon, and cheese. Yield: 10 cups.

"Cottage cheese and sour cream stay fresh longer, if stored upside down."

"Season tomatoes with basil, chives, oregano, or sour cream."

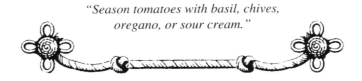

Black Bean Soup

1 pound dried black beans	1 cup chopped green peppers
3 quarts cold water	4 t. minced garlic (about 8 cloves)
3 t. salt	1 T. oregano, crushed
1/4 cup salad oil	1/2 t. ground cumin
1/4 cup olive oil	1/4 t. pepper
1/2 cup chopped onions	2 T. white vinegar

Rice garnish

2 cups cold cooked rice
1/2 cup finely chopped onion
1/3 cup olive oil
2 T. white vinegar
2 T. chopped parsley
1/4 t. salt

Rinse beans with cold water; drain. In dutch oven or large saucepan, add 3 quarts cold water to beans. Heat to boiling, cover and cook 2 minutes. Remove from heat; let stand covered for 1 hour. Add salt to bean mixture and cook over medium heat, stirring occasionally, until beans are tender, about 3 hours. In medium skillet, heat both oils. Add onions and green peppers and saute until tender. Add garlic, oregano, cumin, and pepper. Cook over low heat 3 minutes to blend flavors. Add this mixture to the cooked beans along with the vinegar. Simmer 10 minutes. Allow soup to cool. Purée half the soup, 2 cups at a time. Stir puréed soup back into remaining soup. Reheat over low heat, stirring occasionally. Add water to thin if necessary. Serve with rice garnish. To prepare garnish, combine last 6 ingredients, cover, and refrigerate until serving time. Yield: 10 cups.

Cheese-Pumpkin Soup

¹/₂	cup sliced green onions	¹/₄	t. cinnamon
2	T. butter or margarine	2	cups milk
2	T. all-purpose flour	1	can (10 oz.) chicken broth
1	t. salt	1	can (16 oz.) pumpkin
¹/₂	t. nutmeg	1¹/₂	cups shredded Cheddar cheese

In large saucepan lightly sauté green onions in butter. Stir in flour, salt, nutmeg, and cinnamon. Remove from heat. Add milk and broth. Cook, stirring, about 15 minutes until thickened.

Blend in pumpkin. Simmer 5 minutes longer, stirring frequently. Add cheese. Stir until melted.

Ladle into soup bowls. Top each serving with a slice of tomato, sprinkled with cheese and green onions, if desired. Yield: 6 cups.

Clam Chowder

6	slices bacon	2	(6.5 oz.) cans chopped clams
2	medium onions		salt & pepper to taste
3	large potatoes	4	cups milk

Fry bacon until crisp, remove and crumble. Dice onions and potatoes; put potatoes in cold salted water until ready to use. Sauté onions in bacon fat until transparent. Open cans of clams and turn into soup pot along with onions, potatoes, and bacon; salt and pepper lightly. Add sufficient water to cover. Simmer over low heat until potatoes are done. Add milk and simmer for 15 minutes; do not boil. Yield: 9 cups.

"If soups or stews taste too salty, add a potato.
It will absorb the salt."
"A lettuce leaf dropped in a pot of soup will
absorb the grease from the top."

Cream of Broccoli Soup

1¹/₂ lb. fresh broccoli or
    2 (10 oz.) pkgs. frozen
¹/₄ cup sliced green onions
¹/₂ t. salt

2 cups chicken broth
3 T. butter or margarine
3 T. flour
2 cups milk

In medium saucepan, cook broccoli and seasonings in chicken broth as indicated on package directions or in the microwave (if using fresh broccoli) for 10 minutes on HIGH. Purée in blender or food processor. Set aside.

In a medium saucepan, melt butter. With wire whisk, stir in flour and cook until smooth and bubbly, about 1 minute, stirring constantly. Slowly blend in milk. Bring just to a boil, stirring frequently with whisk.

Stir in puréed broccoli mixture; heat through. Garnish with a dollop of sour cream, if desired. Yield: 6 cups.

Cream of Garlic Soup

3 oz. garlic cloves,
    peeled (about ³/₄ cup)
3 T. olive oil
2¹/₂ cups chicken broth
1 cup dry white wine

2¹/₂ cups whole milk
1 cup whipping cream
1 medium russet potato,
    peeled and coarsely chopped
    salt and white pepper to taste

Blend garlic in processor to chop. Add garlic paste to oil over low heat, cooking for about 12 minutes until beginning to color, stirring frequently. Add broth and wine. Bring to a boil and reduce heat and simmer for 30 minutes. Add milk, cream, and potato and simmer for 30 minutes. Purée soup in blender and return to sauce pan and bring to simmer. Season with salt and white pepper. This soup can be prepared a day ahead and stored covered in the refrigerator. Yield: 6 cups.

Elegant Mushroom Soup

³/₄	cup chopped green onions	2	T. all-purpose flour
2	cups chopped fresh mushrooms	2	cups chicken broth
¹/₄	cup butter or margarine, melted	1	cup milk

Sauté onions and mushrooms in butter in a dutch oven until onions are tender. Stir in flour.

Gradually add chicken broth and milk to mushroom mixture; cook over low heat 10 minutes or just until thoroughly heated. Yield: 4 cups.

"If herbs and spices have no aroma, throw them out and buy a new supply. If you are still using the same herbs you had ten years ago, you might as well be adding a pinch of dust from the vacuum cleaner."

French Market Soup

2	cups of various dry beans	¹/₂	t. each of salt, pepper
	(pinto, northern, lentil, navy,	1	(28 oz.) can tomatoes
	barley, blackeye, lima, etc.)	2	onions, chopped
3	quarts water	1	cup chopped celery
	meaty ham bone	2	cloves garlic, minced
1	T. baking soda	¹/₄	cup parsley, minced

Wash beans and put in heavy pot; cover with water and baking soda and soak overnight. Drain. Add 3 quarts water, ham bone, salt, and pepper. Bring to boil and simmer 2¹/₂ hours. Add remaining ingredients and simmer 45 minutes to one hour. Remove ham bone; cut and chop meat from bone and return to pot. You can add smoked sausage or ¹/₂ cup red wine. This soups improves with age. Yield: 20 cups.

This recipe can also be made by cooking it in a crockpot on low for 8 hours.

French Onion Soup

Heat: **3 cans beef bouillon**

Sauté: **2 large onions, thinly sliced in 1 T. butter**

Add: **1 t. salt and ¹/₄ t. pepper to bouillon. Add onions.**

Grate: **1 lb. Swiss cheese.**

1 loaf French bread

In a large casserole put all but one cup of soup and sprinkle ¹/₂ cup cheese on top. Arrange a layer of toasted bread slices on soup and sprinkle with half of the remaining cheese, then the rest of the bread and the rest of the cheese. Pour the last bit of soup over all. Place in hot 475° oven for 5-7 minutes until cheese is melted and bubbly. Yield: 4 servings.

Gazpacho

9	**medium fresh tomatoes or two 1-pound cans whole tomatoes**
3	**cloves garlic (more or less, to taste)**
1	**large cucumber**
2	**large green peppers**
3	**stalks of celery**
3	**t. salt**
1	**t. black pepper**
¹/₂	**cup bouillon**
¹/₄	**cup dry sherry**
2	**cups tomato or V-8 juice**
4	**slices of bread**
¹/₄	**cup olive oil**

Blend everything but tomato juice in blender or food processor. Put into a storage container and add tomato juice; chill. Serve with the following garnishes: chopped cucumber, chopped green pepper, chopped scallions, and croutons. Yield: 6-8 servings.

Honolulu Academy Chicken Curry Soup

3 cups chopped onion	3 T. each butter, olive oil
4 cloves garlic, minced	1$\frac{1}{2}$-2 t. curry

Sauté together in a 3-quart sauce pan. Process in food processor or blender.

Add and blend:

2 (10$\frac{3}{4}$ oz.) cans cream of potato soup

2 cups clear chicken broth

2 cups sour cream

$\frac{1}{4}$-$\frac{1}{2}$ t. Garden Cafe Spice

Heat for flavors to blend. Stir often. Garnish with parsley, peanuts, sour cream, or mango chutney on top. May also be served cold. Yield: 8 cups.

Garden Cafe Spice

1 bottle Bay leaves

1 bottle Bouquet Garne

$\frac{1}{3}$ bottle Pumpkin Pie Spice

1 t. white pepper

$\frac{1}{2}$ t. each ground cumin and cloves

$\frac{1}{4}$ t. red cayenne pepper

$\frac{1}{8}$ t. garlic powder

Remove stems from bay leaves. Blend until pulverized. Add all but Bouquet Garne. Add last and blend until Bouquet Garne disappears.

Hot and Spicy Chicken Soup

2 cups homemade chicken broth or canned chicken broth
6 slices peeled fresh ginger, about $^1/_4$ inch thick
3 cloves garlic, smashed, peeled and sliced
$^1/_8$ t. hot red-pepper flakes
1 t. Worcestershire sauce
1 T. fresh coriander leaves
2 T. thinly sliced scallion greens
3 t. light soy

In an 8 cup glass measure, combine broth, ginger, garlic, pepper flakes, and Worcestershire sauce. Microwave, uncovered on HIGH for 8 minutes.

Remove from oven and stir in remaining ingredients. Serve hot. Yield: 2 servings.

*"To improve the taste of canned tomatoes, empty
the tomatoes into a bowl and let them 'air' for
an hour before using."*

Minestrone

1 cup celery, chopped
1 cup onion, chopped
1 clove garlic, minced
$^1/_4$ cup oil
$1^1/_2$ t. salt
$^1/_2$ t. pepper
2 quarts water

2 (6 oz.) cans tomato paste
1 cup cabbage, chopped
1 (10 oz.) pkg. of peas and carrots
1 quart beef broth
1 (15 oz.) can kidney beans, drained
1 cup macaroni, uncooked

Sauté onion and garlic in oil. Add all other ingredients except kidney beans and macaroni and simmer one hour. Add kidney beans and macaroni and simmer another 15 minutes. Yield: 10-12 servings.

Pumpkin Soup

2¹/₂	lb. canned or 4 cups freshly cooked pumpkin	1	cup milk
3	T. butter	1	cup cream
1	cup onion, chopped	¹/₄	t. nutmeg
2	cups chicken broth	¹/₈	t. cayenne

Melt butter in heavy saucepan over medium high heat. Add onions and cook until soft, but not browned. Blend in broth and spices and bring to a boil. Add pumpkin. Blend and heat thoroughly. Add milk and cream.

For an added taste, add ¹/₂ cup sherry. Yield: 6-8 servings.

Savory Grouper Stew

1   lb. grouper fillets or other fish fillets
1   cup chopped onion
¹/₃   cup melted margarine or cooking oil
1   can (1 lb. 12 oz.) tomatoes
2   cups diced potatoes
1   cup water
¹/₄   cup ketchup
¹/₂   t. salt
     pepper to taste
1   pkg. (1 lb.) mixed vegetables

Cut fillets into pieces about 1 inch square. In a 3 qt. saucepan, sauté onion in margarine or oil until tender. Add tomatoes, potatoes, water, ketchup, salt, and pepper to taste. Cover and simmer 30 min. Add fish, mixed vegetables. Cover and simmer for about 15 minutes longer, or until the potatoes are tender and fish flakes easily when tested with a fork. Makes 6 servings. Serve with sourdough bread. Yield: 6 servings.

She-Crab Soup

1	lb. crabmeat with roe, if possible	$^1/_4$	t. celery salt
2	T. butter	1	T. Worcestershire sauce
2	T. flour		salt and pepper to taste
$2^1/_2$	cups half and half		Sherry

Melt butter on low heat and blend in flour until smooth. Add half and half slowly. Add celery salt and Worcestershire sauce. Add crabmeat. Adjust to taste. Add about 1 t. warm sherry to bottom of each bowl of soup. Yield: 4-6 servings.

"To freeze all kinds of fresh berries: place on a wax paper covered cookie sheet in a single layer, freeze for one hour, put in airtight plastic bags and fasten securely."
"Freeze extra egg whites in an ice cube tray. Store them in a plastic bag in the freezer. They will thaw quickly."

Strawberry Soup

2	cups puréed strawberries	$^1/_2$	cup ice water
$^1/_2$	cup sour cream, buttermilk, or plain yogurt	1	T. lemon juice
$^1/_2$	cup sugar	1	T. lemon peel, grated
$^1/_2$	cup white wine	$^1/_2$	t. or less cinnamon
1	cup orange juice	$^1/_2$	t. or less allspice

Combine ingredients. Blend in blender or food processor. Serve cold. Yield: 6-8 servings.

Tomato-Ginger Soup

1	medium onion, quartered	¹/₂	cup chicken consommé
2¹/₂	oz. peeled fresh ginger	1	T. sugar
1	(28 oz.) can Italian style		salt & white pepper to taste
	tomatoes or 1 pound fresh	1	cup cream
¹/₂	cup unsalted butter	2	egg yolks

Purée onion and ginger in food processor. Set aside. Purée tomatoes. Melt butter, sauté onion purée about 4 minutes. Add tomato purée, consommé and spices. Bring to boil. Add cream, simmer to reduce about 30 minutes.

Beat egg yolks in small bowl. Gradually add about 1 cup hot soup. Return all to soup pan. Heat to thicken, about 2 mintues. Strain soup through fine sieve or folley food mill. Rewarm soup. Adjust seasonings. Yield: 4-6 servings.

Tortilla Soup

3	T. corn oil	2	bay leaves
4	corn tortillas, coarsely chopped	8	cups chicken stock
6	cloves garlic, finely chopped	1	cooked chicken breast,
1	T. chopped fresh cilantro		cut in strips
1	cup fresh onion purée	1	avocado, peeled, seeded & cubed
2	cups fresh tomato purée	1	cup shredded Cheddar cheese
1	T. cumin powder	3	corn tortillas, cut into thin strips
2	t. chili powder		and fried crisp
	salt & cayenne pepper to taste		

Heat oil in a large saucepan over medium heat. Sauté tortillas with garlic and cilantro over medium heat until tortillas are soft. Add onion and fresh tomato purée and bring to a boil. Add cumin, chili powder, bay leaves, and chicken stock. Bring to a boil again, then reduce heat to simmer. Add salt and cayenne pepper to taste and cook, stirring frequently, for 30 minutes. Skim fat from surface and serve with an equal portion of chicken breast, avocado, shredded cheese, and crisp tortilla strips. Serve immediately. May be made one day ahead. Yield: 8 servings.

Vichyssoise

4	leeks or 1 large bunch green onions
1	large onion
¼	cup butter or margarine
3	large potatoes
4	cups chicken broth
½	pint whipping cream
1	cup milk
1	t. salt
¼	t. white pepper
	Chopped chives or green onion tops for garnish

Split leeks in half lengthwise so you can wash thoroughly; then cut in 1 inch lengths; discard tough green tops. Or cut white part of green onions in 1 inch lengths. Using the metal blade of the food processor, process leek with on-off bursts until coarsely chopped. Place in a 3 quart kettle.

Cut onions in chunks and process with on-off bursts until coarsely chopped. Add to leeks along with butter and cook over low heat until onion is soft but not browned.

Peel potatoes, cut in chunks, and process, one at a time, with on-off bursts until coarsely chopped. Add to onion mixture along with chicken broth. Bring to a boil; then reduce heat, cover, and simmer until potatoes are tender (about 20 minutes).

Still using metal blade, process ½ of the soup at a time until smooth. Pour puréed soup into a bowl, stir in cream and milk, then season with salt and pepper. If too thick, thin with additional milk. Chill thoroughly. Serve cold, sprinkled with chives or green onion tops. Easy to make a day ahead. Yield: 6 servings.

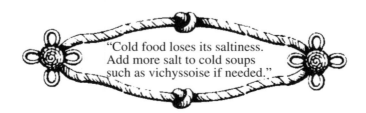

"Cold food loses its saltiness.
Add more salt to cold soups
such as vichyssoise if needed."

Breads

The Seven Subs in Dry Dock.
Navy Yard. Charleston. S.C.
After Flooding
Photo by Hildebrandt.
Passed by The Chief Naval Censor

Breads

Apple-Banana Bread

Banana Nut Bread

Basic White Bread • Beer Bread

Bread Sticks • Breakfast Casserole

Chocolate-Almond Zucchini Bread

Cottage Cheese Buns • Crispy Cracker Bread

English Muffin Loaves • Flour Tortillas

Food Processor Pizza

French Bread • Funnel Cakes • Granola

Hawaiian Sweet Bread

Hot Cakes

Irish Soda Bread

Karl's Oat Bran Muffins

Lavosh • Lemon Muffins

Norwegian Lefse

Norwegian Pancakes

Old Fashioned Potato Loaves

Parker House Rolls • Pita Crisps

Potato Doughnuts • Pull-Apart Loaves

Quick Yeast Rolls • Raised Doughnuts

Zucchini Bread

Apple-Banana Bread

1	cup apple juice concentrate	1¹/₂	cups whole-wheat flour
¹/₃	cup margarine	¹/₂	cup wheat germ
2	eggs	1	t. baking soda
2	medium bananas, mashed	¹/₂	t. salt
1	t. vanilla		

Heat oven to 350°. Grease a 9 x 5 x 3 inch loaf pan. Melt apple juice concentrate and butter in a small saucepan over medium-low heat. When butter is almost melted, remove from heat and stir until completely melted. Whisk in eggs and vanilla. Stir in mashed bananas. Combine flour, wheat germ, baking soda, and salt. Add flour mixture to juice mixture. Stir. Pour into greased loaf pan. Bake 55-60 minutes. Yield: 1 loaf.

Banana Nut Bread

¹/₂	cup sugar
¹/₂	cup shortening
2	eggs
1³/₄	cups all-purpose flour
1	t. baking powder
¹/₂	t. soda
¹/₂	t. salt
1	cup mashed ripe banana
¹/₂	cup chopped walnuts

Cream together sugar and shortening; add eggs and beat well. Add dry ingredients alternately with the banana, blending well after each addition. Stir in nuts. Pour into greased 9¹/₂ x 5 x 3 inch loaf pan. Bake at 350° for 40 minutes or until done. Remove from pan and cool on rack. Yield: 1 loaf.

Basic White Bread

$^1/_2$ **cup milk**

3   **T. sugar**

2   **t. salt**

3   **T. butter or margarine**

1   **pkg. active dry yeast**

1$^1/_2$ **cups warm water (105°-115°)**

5-6   **cups bread flour**

Scald milk. Stir in 2 T. sugar, 3 T. butter or margarine, and 2 t. salt. Cool to lukewarm. Dissolve yeast and 1 T. sugar in warm water. Proof for 10 minutes to make sure the yeast is "active and alive." Add lukewarm milk mixture and 4 $^1/_2$ cups flour.

If you have a KitchenAid mixer: Turn to Speed 2 for 2 minutes or until well blended. Continuing on Speed 2, add remaining flour, $^1/_2$ cup at a time, until dough clings to hook and cleans sides of bowl, about 3 mintues. Knead on speed 2 for 7 to 10 minutes longer, or until dough is smooth and elastic. Stop. Dough will be slightly sticky to the touch.

If making without a KitchenAid Mixer: Mix together with a wooden spoon. When blended, remove dough from bowl and knead with your hands for 15 minutes, adding 1 cup flour as needed. Dough will be slightly sticky.

Place in greased bowl, turning to grease top. Cover; let rise in warm place, free from draft, until doubled in bulk, about one hour. Punch down. Let rest for 15 minutes. Divide dough in half. Shape each half into a loaf. Place each loaf in a greased 9 x 5 x 2 inch bread pan. Cover; let rise in warm place, free from draft, until doubled in bulk, about one hour.

Bake at 400° for 30 minutes or until done. Remove from pans, spread about $^1/_2$ T. butter over top of each loaf; cool on wire racks. Yield: 2 Loaves.

Crispy Cracker Bread

1/4 oz. pkg. active dry yeast	3 T. butter or margarine, melted
1 cup warm water (105°-115°)	1 1/2-3 cups all-purpose flour
2 t. sugar	1 egg, slightly beaten
1 t. salt	sesame seeds

Heat oven to 400°. In large bowl, dissolve yeast in warm water. Stir in sugar, salt, and butter. Gradually stir in flour, 1 cup at a time, using enough flour to make dough easy to handle. Turn dough onto lighly floured surface; knead until smooth (5 min.). Divide dough into 4 equal portions; shape into balls. Let rest 10 minutes; roll each ball into 12 inch circle. Place on greased cookie sheets. Brush with beaten egg; sprinkle with salt, pepper, or sesame seed. Bake for 10-15 mintues or until lightly browned. Cool completely on wire rack. (Bread will be irregular in shape and browning.) To serve, break into pieces. Freezes easily.

English Muffin Loaves

6 cups all-purpose flour, divided	1/4 t. baking soda
2 pkg. dry yeast	2 cups milk
1 T. sugar	1/2 cup water
1 1/2 t. salt	Cornmeal

Combine 3 cups flour, yeast, sugar, salt, and soda in a large mixing bowl; set aside. Combine milk and water in a small saucepan; heat until very warm (120-130°). Gradually add milk mixture to dry ingredients, mixing on low speed of electric mixer 2-3 minutes. Stir in enough remaining flour to make a soft dough. Divide dough in half; shape each half into a loaf. Grease two 8 1/2 x 4 1/2 x 3 inch loaf pans; sprinkle bottom and sides with cornmeal. Place dough into prepared pans; sprinkle with cornmeal.

Cover and let rise in a warm place (85°), free from drafts, 45 minutes or until doubled in bulk. Bake at 400° for 25 minutes. Yield: 2 loaves.

Flour Tortillas

- **4 cups flour**
- **2 t. salt**
- **$^1/_8$ t. baking powder**
- **$^2/_3$ cup shortening**
- **1 cup plus 3 T. hot water**

Stir together flour, salt, and baking powder. Cut in shortening with a pastry-blender or blending fork until pieces are size of tiny peas. Add water and mix into a ball. Shape into $1^1/_2$ inch balls. Roll out into very thin 6 inch circles.

Place on an ungreased skillet (375°) and fry 2 minutes on each side. Cover with a towel to keep the tortillas from drying out. Yield: 2 dozen.

Food Processor Pizza

1 cup water	**1 green pepper, thinly sliced**
2 T. shortening	**8 ounces, mozzarella cheese**
3$^1/_4$ cups all-purpose flour, unsifted	**or jack cheese, grated**
2 T. sugar	**1 small onion, coarsely chopped**
1 t. salt	**1 can black olives,**
1 pkg. active dry yeast	**drained, thinly sliced**
1 egg, room temperature	**$^1/_4$ cup grated Parmesan cheese**
2 T. olive oil or salad oil	**$^1/_2$ lb. salami, pepperoni,**
$^1/_4$ pound mushrooms, thinly sliced	**thinly sliced**

In a small pan, heat water and shortening just until shortening melts; remove from heat and let stand until tepid (110°). In food processor, using metal blade, process $1^1/_2$ cups of the flour, sugar, salt, and yeast for 2 seconds to mix. With motor running, pour shortening mixture slowly through the feed tube. Add egg and process for 2 seconds to mix. Sprinkle over another $1^1/_2$ cups of the flour and process until dough forms a ball.

Sprinkle remaining $^1/_4$ cup flour on a board, turn dough onto it, and knead until smooth and elastic and most of flour has been absorbed (3-4 minutes). Divide dough

in half. Pull and stretch each piece of dough to form a 12 inch circle; then transfer each piece onto a 12 inch greased pizza pan. (If time is not short, let dough rest for 30 minutes before shaping; this eliminates elasticity). Rub 1 T. oil over each pan of dough and let stand in a warm place while you prepare topping. Yield: 2-12" crusts.

Tomato Sauce:

In food processor, using metal blade, process **2 cloves garlic** until chopped. Cut **1 large onion** into chunks, add to garlic, and process with on-off bursts until finely chopped. Heat **2 T. salad oil** in a wide frying pan over medium-high heat, add onion mixture, and stirring occasionally, cook until golden (about 5 minutes). Remove pan from heat and stir in **2 cans (6 oz. each) tomato paste**, **1 t. salt**, **¹/₂ t. each marjoram**, **thyme, oregano leaves,** and **dry basil**. Makes enough sauce to cover 2 pizzas.

To assemble pizza, spread tomato sauce over dough. Arrange mushroom, salami and green pepper over sauce. Sprinkle onion, olives, and cheeses over all.

Bake one pizza at a time on lowest rack of a 500° oven until crust is browned (7-10 minutes). Cut hot pizza in wedges to serve.

USS L. Mendel Rivers

French Bread

2¹/₂	cups warm water (105°-115°)	7	cups flour
2	pkgs. active dry yeast	¹/₄	cup corn meal
1	T. salt	1	egg white
1	T. butter or margarine, melted	1	T. cold water

Dissolve yeast in warm water in warmed bowl. Add salt, margarine and flour. Turn to speed 2 on mixer and mix until well blended, about 2 minutes. Continue to beat for 2 minutes longer. Stop. Dough will be sticky.

Place in greased bowl, turning to grease top. Let rise in warm place, free from draft, until doubled in bulk, about 1 hour.

Punch dough down and divide dough into 2 equal parts; roll each into a 12 x 15 inch oblong. Roll up tightly beginning at long side, sealing as you roll. Taper ends if desired. Place loaves on 2 greased baking sheets, which have been sprinkled with cornmeal. Cover; let rise in a warm place, free from draft, until doubled in bulk, about 1 hour.

With sharp knife, make 4 diagonal cuts on top of each loaf. Bake at 450° for 25 minutes. Remove from oven and brush with slightly beaten egg white and water. Return to oven and bake 5 minutes longer. Remove from baking sheets and cool on wire racks. Yield: 2 loaves.

Funnel Cakes

1¹/₄	cups flour	³/₄	cup milk
2	T. sugar	1	egg, beaten
1	t. baking powder		oil
¹/₄	t. salt		powdered sugar

Combine dry ingredients. Add combined milk and egg, mixing until smooth. Holding finger over opening, fill a ¹/₂-inch funnel with ¹/₄ cup batter. Place funnel near oil; remove finger and pour batter into 1 inch of hot oil using circular motion to form 4 inch spiral. Fry until golden brown, turning once, drain on paper towels. Sprinkle with powdered sugar. Serve warm. Yield: 6-8 servings.

Granola

  ¹/₄   **cup safflower oil**

  ¹/₂   **cup honey**

  ¹/₂   **t. vanilla extract**

   4   **cups old-fashioned rolled oats**

   1   **cup wheat germ**

   1   **cup sliced almonds**

   1   **cup hulled sunflower seed**

  ¹/₂   **cup sesame seed**

  ¹/₂   **cup whole-wheat bran**

In saucepan, heat first 3 ingredients. Add to remaining ingredients in bowl and stir thoroughly. Spread on 2 oiled cookie sheets and bake in preheated 325° oven, stirring twice during baking to prevent over-browning, about 15 minutes. Store airtight in cool dry place. Yield: 2 quarts.

Hawaiian Sweet Bread

3	**eggs, room temperature**		1	**t. corn oil**
1	**package yeast**		6	**T. margarine, melted**
¹/₄	**t. lemon extract**		³/₄	**cup sugar**
¹/₂	**t. vanilla**		5-6	**cups flour**
¹/₂	**cup milk, scalded**		¹/₂	**t. salt**
¹/₄	**t. nutmeg**			

Dissolve yeast in ¹/₂ cup warm water. Beat eggs and combine with yeast, lemon extract, vanilla, milk, nutmeg, corn oil, margarine, and sugar. Beat well. Add 4¹/₂ cups flour and knead until dough no longer sticks to bowl. Add remaining flour as you knead. Cover and let rise until size has doubled, about 2 hours. Punch dough down and divide into 2 even mounds. Place in greased pie tins. Cover and let rise, about 5 hours. Bake 45 minutes at 300°. Yield: 2 loaves.

Hot Cakes

  1   **cup flour**
  1   **T. sugar**
  1   **t. baking soda**
 ¼   **t. salt**
  1   **egg**
1½   **cups buttermilk**

Mix all ingredients together. Stir in **2 T. melted butter or vegetable oil**. Set electric skillet to 350° and make Hot Cakes. Tastes like sourdough pancakes. Yield: 4 servings.

Irish Soda Bread

  2   **cups sifted flour**
1½   **t. baking powder**
 ¾   **t. baking soda**
  1   **t. salt**
  3   **T. sugar**
1½   **t. caraway**
  3   **T. shortening**

Blend first six ingredients and with a pastry blender cut in shortening.
Add:

  1   **cup buttermilk**
 ⅔   **cup raisins**

Mix, knead, and put into a greased 9" round pan. Melt **¼ cup butter** and brush over loaf after making an X on loaf. Sprinkle with sugar. Bake at 350° for 30 minutes. Yield: 1 loaf.

Karl's Oat Bran Muffins

- **2¹/₄ cups oat bran**
- **¹/₄ cup brown sugar**
- **¹/₄ cup walnuts**
- **¹/₄ cup raisins**
- **1 T. baking powder**
- **¹/₂ t. salt**
- **³/₄ cup milk**
- **¹/₄ cup liquid egg substitute**
- **¹/₄ cup honey**
- **2 T. sunflower oil**

Mix all the above and put into a greased muffin pan or use paper liners. Bake at 425° for 15 minutes. Yield: 1 dozen.

Lavosh

- **2³/₄ cups flour**
- **¹/₂ t. baking soda**
- **¹/₂ t. salt**
- **¹/₄ cup sugar**
- **¹/₂ cup butter**
- **1 cup buttermilk**
- **1 T. sesame seeds**
- **1 T. poppy seeds**

Preheat oven to 375°. Sift dry ingredients together. With an electric beater, blend in butter. Add the two kinds of seeds and buttermilk and mix until batter forms a big ball. Pinch off tablespoon size balls of dough. Flour a cutting board; roll out each ball of dough until thin. Pick up rolled dough on rolling pin and place on cookie sheet. Repeat process of flouring the board and rolling dough. Bake each batch for 8-10 minutes or until golden brown. Make ahead and freeze in a ziptop bag. Yield: approximately 60 servings.

Lemon Muffins

2 cups all-purpose flour	$^{1}/_{2}$ cup butter
$^{1}/_{2}$ cup plus 2 T. sugar	$^{1}/_{2}$ cup fresh lemon juice
1 T. baking powder	2 eggs
1 t. salt	rind of 1 lemon, grated

Butter muffin tins inside and on top. Combine all dry ingredients less 2 T. sugar. Melt butter; off heat stir in lemon juice, eggs, and rind. Stir egg mixture into dry and blend till well moistened. Spoon into cups and sprinkle tops with sugar. Bake for 15-20 minutes at 400°. Yield: 1 dozen.

Norwegian Lefse

3 medium potatoes, peeled and quartered (1 lb.)

2 T. butter or margarine, softened

1 T. milk

$^{1}/_{2}$ t. salt

1 cup all-purpose flour

In a saucepan cook potatoes in boiling water about 20 minutes or until soft and tender. Drain well; shake potatoes in pan over low heat to dry. Remove pan from heat. Mash with potato masher, electric mixer, or put through ricer. Measure 2 cups.

Beat together the potatoes, butter, milk, and salt; cover and chill thoroughly. Turn mixture out onto a lightly floured surface. Sprinkle with half of the flour. Knead for 8-10 minutes gradually kneading in remaining flour. Divide dough into 16 portions; shape each into a ball.

On a floured surface roll each ball to a 6 inch paper-thin round. Cook on hot, greased skillet or griddle 2-3 minutes on each side or until lightly browned.

Spread with butter and sprinkle with sugar and cinnamon. Fold each one in half and then half again. Serve. Yield: 6-8 servings.

Norwegian Pancakes

3	eggs
1¼	cups milk
¾	cup flour
1	T. sugar
½	t. salt

In an electric blender beat eggs until thick and lemon-colored. Add milk on low speed. Add dry ingredients, mixing until smooth. Pour ¼ cup of batter onto moderately hot buttered griddle. Cook as you would a crepe. Turn when underside is light brown. Fold in half and then half again and remove to a warm platter. Keep pancakes in warm oven, covered with a towel, until all are made. Serve with butter, maple syrup, or powdered sugar. Yield: 4 servings.

Old Fashioned Potato Loaves

1	medium potato	1	T. salt
2	pkgs. yeast	1	cup warm milk
2	T. margarine	6½-7½	cups flour
2	T. sugar		

Peel and dice potato; boil until tender. Drain, reserving liquid to make 1 cup. Cool to 105°-115°. Mash potato, set aside.

Sprinkle yeast in potato water and dissolve. Add margarine, sugar, salt, potato, warm milk, and 3 cups flour. Stir and add additional flour to make stiff dough. Knead 10 minutes. Place in greased bowl, cover, and let rise in warm place until doubled, about 50 minutes. Punch down, turn, cover, and let rise 20 minutes. Punch down, shape into loaves, cover, and let rise until doubled.

Bake 375° on a greased cookie sheet for 35-40 minutes. Yield: 2 loaves.

Parker House Rolls

1½ t. dry yeast	1 t. salt
¾ cup warm water	1 t. sugar
½ cup scalded milk	2 T. butter
3 cups bread flour	

Dissolve yeast in ¼ cup warm water. In a large mixing bowl, combine the remaining water with scalded milk, salt, sugar, and 1 T. butter; blend well.

Add yeast. Add flour, one cup at a time. Mix dough with a dough hook or by hand for about 5 minutes. Cover bowl with a damp cloth and let rise in a warm place until doubled in bulk, about 1-1½ hours.

Shape dough by hand into 24 2" balls and arrange in a single layer in a buttered baking dish, cover, and let rise in a warm place for 30 minutes or until doubled in size. Let remaining tablespoon of butter soften.

Using the floured handle of a wooden spoon, press each ball through the center until almost cut in half. Brush the crease with a little of the soft butter and press halves together like a purse; repeat with each roll. Let rise again until doubled in bulk. Bake on middle shelf of 400° oven for 15 minutes. Serve warm. Yield: 2 dozen.

Spring Dinner for Eight

Vichyssoise, page 46
Green Salad with Lo-Cal Salad Dressing, page 88
Parker House Rolls, page 62
Flank Steak, Slices, page 144
Broccoli with Fresh Mushrooms, page 96
Red Potatoes — Mashed, page 108
Sherry Bundt Cake, page 185

Pita Crisps

3 large pita bread rounds	¹/₈ t. garlic powder
¹/₄ cup margarine, melted	¹/₈ t. onion powder
1 T. dried parsley flakes	¹/₄ cup grated Parmesan
1 t. dried oregano, crushed	or Romano cheese

Separate each pita bread into 2 round single layers. In a small mixing bowl, stir together margarine, parsley, oregano, garlic powder, and onion powder. Brush a scant tablespoon of the mixture on the rough side of each pita half.

Sprinkle 2 t. cheese over each pita round. Cut each round into 6 wedges. Arrange wedges in single layer on ungreased baking sheets. Bake in a 350° oven for 12-15 minutes or until crisp and golden brown. Serve warm or at room temperature. Yield: 4-6 servings.

Potato Doughnuts

1 pkg. dry yeast	2 eggs
1¹/₂ cups water	1 t. salt
²/₃ cup shortening	1 cup hot mashed potatoes
²/₃ cup sugar	7-7¹/₂ cups flour

Dissolve yeast in lukewarm water and set aside. Cream shortening and sugar, add eggs and salt. Beat well. Blend in potatoes. Add yeast mixture gradually. Add flour, beating well after each addition. Knead until smooth and satiny. Let rise in greased, covered bowl until doubled. Divide in half. Roll out ¹/₂ inch thickness. Cut out with cutter and let rise until doubled. Fry at 375° until golden (1 minute each side). Dip in glaze while warm. Yield: 2 dozen.

Glaze:

Gradually add ¹/₂ **cup boiling water** to **3 cups sifted powdered sugar**. Stir in **1 t. vanilla**.

Pull-Apart Loaves

3	T. sugar	5½-6½	cups unsifted flour	
2	t. salt	1	pkg. active dry yeast	
1½	cups water	3	T. margarine, melted	
½	cup milk			

In a large bowl thoroughly mix 2 cups flour, sugar, salt, and undissolved active dry yeast. Combine water, milk, and 3 T. margarine in a saucepan. Heat over low until liquids are very warm (120°-130°). Gradually add to dry ingredients and beat 2 minutes at medium speed, scraping bowl occasionally. Add ¾ cup flour. Stir in enough additional flour to make a stiff dough. Turn out onto lightly floured board. Knead until smooth and elastic, about 8-10 minutes. Place in greased bowl, turning to grease top. Cover. Let rise in warm place free from draft until doubled in bulk, about 1 hour.

Punch dough down; divide in half. Cover. Let rest 15 minutes. Roll one half to a 12 x 8 inch rectangle. Brush with melted margarine. Cut into 6 equal pieces. Place on edge in greased 8 x 4 x 2 inch loaf pan so that layers form one long row down length of pan. Repeat with remaining dough. Cover; let rise in warm place, free from draft, until doubled in bulk, about 1 hour. Bake at 400° about 30 minutes or until done. Remove from pans and cool on wire rackes. Yield: 2 loaves.

Autumn Dinner for Eight

Cheese and Pumpkin Soup, page 37
Tangy Romaine Salad, page 79
Pull-Apart Loaves, page 64
Chicken and Artichoke Casserole, page 128
Fried Rice, page 100
Garnish with oranges slices and parsley
Marble-ous Frozen Peanut Butter Dessert, page 166

Quick Yeast Rolls

2   pkgs. dry yeast in 1$^{1}/_{4}$ cups warm water
$^{1}/_{4}$ cup sugar
1$^{1}/_{4}$ t. salt
1   egg
3   cups flour
2   t. shortening (oil)

Dissolve yeast in water. Sift together dry ingredients. Mix all together and let rise 10 minutes. Dough will be sticky. Grease muffin tins. Fill $^{1}/_{2}$ full and let rise 20 minutes. Bake at 400° for 20 minutes. Yield: 1 dozen.

For variation: add $^{1}/_{4}$-$^{1}/_{2}$ t. cinnamon to dough.

Raised Doughnuts

2   cups milk, scalded
$^{1}/_{3}$ cup sugar
1   T. salt
1   pkg. yeast

$^{1}/_{3}$ cup lukewarm water
1   egg
5-6   cups flour

Combine the first three ingredients in a mixing bowl. Cool to lukewarm.

Sprinkle yeast over lukewarm water (110°); stir to dissolve. Add yeast mixture, egg, and flour to milk mixture. Beat with mixer at medium speed, about 2 minutes. Gradually stir in enough extra flour to make a soft dough that leaves the sides of the bowl. Turn out on floured surface and knead until smooth and satiny, about 5 minutes.

Place dough in lightly greased bowl. Turn over to grease top. Cover and let rise 1 hour. Roll dough out to $^{1}/_{2}$ inch thickness. Cut with floured 2$^{1}/_{2}$ inch doughnut cutter. Place on floured waxed paper. Cover and let rise until doubled, about 30 minutes.

Pour oil into skillet about 3" deep. Heat to 360°. Fry 2-3 minutes turning once. Drain on paper towels. Roll in sugar. Yield: 3 dozen.

Zucchini Bread

3 cups all-purpose flour	2 cups sugar
1 t. baking powder	1 cup vegetable oil
1 t. baking soda	2 t. vanilla extract
1 t. salt	2 cups shredded zucchini
1 T. ground cinnamon	1 cup chopped pecans
3 eggs	

Combine first 5 ingredients; set aside. Combine eggs, sugar, oil, and vanilla in a large bowl; beat at medium speed of an electric mixer until well blended. Stir in zucchini and pecans. Add remaining dry ingredients, stirring just until moistened.

Spoon batter into 3 greased and floured 1 pound coffee cans. Bake at 350° for 55-60 minutes or until a wooden pick inserted in center comes out clean. Cool in cans 10 minutes; remove to wire rack and cool completely. Serve with whipped cream cheese sprinkled with pecans. Yield: 3 loaves.

For mini-loaves, spoon batter into 7 greased and floured 12 ounce tomato juice cans. Bake at 350° for 35-40 minutes or until a wooden pick inserted in center comes out clean.

Salads

Submarine Squadron 18, Naval Weapons Station, Charleston, SC.
USS Holland tending five Fleet Ballistic Missle Submarines.

Salads

Banana Salad — Oahu Style

Christmas Salad

Cottage Cheese Salad • Crab Salad

Curried Chicken Salad

Five Cup Salad

Fresh Broccoli Salad

Fresh Minted Fruit Salad

Frozen Fruit Salad • Fruit Salad

Grape Salad • 9-Day Cole Slaw

Make Ahead Caesar Salad

Marinated Zucchini Salad

Mushroom Salad

Pasta and Shrimp Salad

Pea Salad • Peas and Peanuts

Pepperoni and Broccoli Salad

Pesto Potato Salad • Pesto Tortellini Salad

Seafoam Lime Mold • Seafood Mold

Spinach Salad • Taco Salad

Tangy Romaine Salad

Tropical Lobster Salad • Vegetable Salad

Wild Rice and Turkey Salad

Banana Salad — Oahu Style

1 egg	1¹/₂ T. vinegar
1 cup sugar	3 bananas, sliced
3 T. water	

Bring the first four ingredients to a boil. Cool and refrigerate. Pour over sliced bananas when ready to serve. Top with nuts and coconut. Yield: 4 servings.

Christmas Salad

2 (3 oz.) pkgs. lime Jello. Mix according to package directions and refrigerate to set in a 9 x 13 inch pan.

1 (3 oz.) pkg. lemon Jello — mix with 1 cup boiling water. While still hot,

2 cups tiny marshmallows should be added; stir until dissolved. Cool.

Mix together:

¹/₄ cup cold water	1 cup heavy cream, whipped
1 small can crushed pineapple, drained	1 (3 oz.) pkg. cream cheese, softened
¹/₂ cup sugar	

Blend with lemon Jello mixture and pour over lime layer and let set until hard (overnight).

2 (3 oz.) pkgs. cherry Jello. Mix according to package directions and pour over as third layer. Set until hard.

Yield: 10-12 servings.

Cottage Cheese Salad

Blend together:

³/₄ **cup boiling water**	¹/₃ **cup lemon juice**
1 **(3 oz.) pkg. of lime Jello**	

Add:

1 **small can crushed pineapple**	2 **cups cottage cheese**

Whip: **1 envelope Dream Whip**. Fold all ingredients in and let set. Refrigerate. Serve the next day. Yield: 4-6 servings.

Crab Salad

¹/₂ **cup French dressing**	¹/₄ **cup mayonnaise**
¹/₃ **cup chili sauce**	4 **cups fresh crab**

Mix the first 3 ingredients together and add to fresh crab for a delicious entree. Yield: 4-6 servings.

Curried Chicken Salad

1 **(8 oz.) can chunk pineapple**	²/₃ **cup mayonnaise**
4 **cups diced cooked chicken**	1 **T. Dijon mustard**
¹/₄ **cup chopped celery**	³/₄ **t. curry powder**
2 **T. chopped green onions**	¹/₈ **t. salt**
¹/₃ **cup toasted slivered almonds**	**lettuce leaves**
¹/₃ **cup raisins**	**pineapple slices**

Drain pineapple, reserving 2 T. juice. Combine pineapple, chicken, and add next 4 ingredients.

Combine reserved pineapple juice, mayonnaise, and next 3 ingredients; add to chicken mixture, and toss well. Cover and chill. Serve on lettuce. Garnish with pineapple slices. Yield: 5 servings.

Grape Salad

Mix and let congeal in a 9 x 13 inch dish:

2	small pkgs. grape Jello (or raspberry Jello)	1	small can crushed pineapple, drained
2	cups boiling water	1	can blueberry pie filling

Mix and spread on top:

1	(8 oz.) pkg. cream cheese	¹/₂	cup sugar
¹/₂	cup sour cream	1	t. vanilla

Yield: 10-12 servings.

9 Day Cole Slaw

3	lb. cabbage (shredded)	1	cup salad oil
1	green pepper (shredded)	1	cup distilled vinegar
1	large onion (shredded)	2	t. salt
2	T. celery seed	2	cups sugar

Mix together shredded cabbage, green pepper and onion. Boil remaining ingredients together and pour over cabbage mixture. Let set in refrigerator for 24 hours. Will keep in the refrigerator for about 9 days. Yield: 18-20 servings.

Make Ahead Caesar Salad

1	garlic clove, crushed	1	T. lemon juice
¹/₄	t. salt	¹/₄	cup oil
¹/₄	t. pepper	2-3	T. Parmesan cheese, grated
¹/₂	t. dry mustard		

Mix all ingredients in bottom of wooden salad bowl. On top, put cut up **romaine lettuce.** DO NOT TOSS. Cover with foil and let stand several hours in refrigerator. Add **tomato wedges** and toss. Serve immediately. Yield: 4-6 servings.

Marinated Zucchini Salad

Marinade:

²/₃	cup salad oil	³/₄	t. salt
¹/₄	cup vinegar	³/₄	t. dry mustard
1	small garlic, minced		dash black pepper
1	t. sugar		

Combine the above and pour over:

2	cups sliced carrots (parboiled)	1	medium zucchini,
1	(14 oz.) can artichokes		(2 cups) thinly sliced

Chill overnight. Serve drained vegetables on **bib lettuce** with **blue cheese**, crumbled. Yield: 6-8 servings.

Mushroom Salad

1   cup salad oil
¹/₃   cup wine vinegar
1   T. lemon juice
¹/₂   t. salt
¹/₄   t. Tabasco
1   small clove garlic, minced
1   T. chopped chives
1   (3 oz.) can chopped mushrooms, drained
6   cups torn head lettuce
1   cup torn spinach leaves
¹/₃   cup sliced pitted ripe olives

In a jar or bowl combine first 8 ingredients. Shake or beat to mix.

In a large bowl combine lettuce, spinach, and olives. Add ³/₄ cup dressing and toss lightly to mix well. Refrigerate remaining dressing in a covered container and reserve for later use. Yield: 6-8 servings.

Pasta and Shrimp Salad

2	lbs. unpeeled fresh shrimp	1	cup sliced water chestnuts
3	cups boiling water	1¹/₂	cups mayonnaise
²/₃	(16 oz.) pkg. vermicelli	3	T. sugar
1	cup diced celery	2	T. vinegar
1	cup sliced ripe olives	³/₄	t. salt
1	cup sliced fresh mushrooms	¹/₄	t. pepper

Add shrimp to boiling water. Cover, turn off heat, and simmer for 5 minutes. Drain and rinse with cold water. Peel and devein shrimp. Cook vermicelli according to package directions; rinse with cold water, drain. Combine shrimp, vermicelli. Add celery, olives, mushrooms, and water chestnuts.

Combine mayonnaise, sugar, vinegar, salt, pepper; pour over pasta mixture and toss until coated. Cover salad and chill. Yield: 8 servings.

"A hollowed out pineapple makes an attractive container for fruit dip. Use a hollowed out watermelon for the fruit."

Pea Salad

Combine and refrigerate overnight:

¹/₂	cup sour cream	1¹/₂	t. sugar
3	T. red wine vinegar	¹/₂	t. salt
4	t. milk	¹/₄	t. garlic powder

Combine and toss with sour cream mixture next day: Yield: 6 servings.

1	(10 oz.) pkg. frozen peas	¹/₄	cup thinly sliced green onions
³/₄	cup sliced water chestnuts	6	bacon slices, cooked and crumbled

Peas and Peanuts

1 (10) oz. box frozen peas

10 oz. Spanish peanuts

2 T. finely chopped onion

¹/₂ cup mayonnaise thinned with a small amount of lemon juice

Mix all ingredients and chill for several hours or overnight. Yield: 6 servings.

Pepperoni and Broccoli Salad

1 pkg. Italian salad dressing mix   **1 cup diced Swiss cheese**

1 lb. fresh broccoli   **¹/₂ lb. fresh mushrooms, sliced**

1 green pepper, chopped   **3¹/₂ oz. sliced pepperoni**

Prepare dressing mix according to package directions and set aside. Trim off large leaves of broccoli. Wash and break off flowerets; reserve stalks for use in other recipes. Combine broccoli and next 4 ingredients in large bowl. Pour dressing over salad; toss gently. Cover and refrigerate 8 hours or overnight. Yield: 6-8 servings.

Pesto Potato Salad

6 potatoes, cooked and cubed

¹/₂ cup chopped onion

¹/₄ cup chopped green bell pepper

2 hard-cooked eggs, chopped

¹/₂ cup pesto (page 157)

Toss all ingredients together. Serve cold or at room temperature. Yield: 8 servings.

Pesto Tortellini Salad

1   lb. frozen or fresh cheese tortellini

Cook tortellini according to directions on package.

Mix together:

- **¹/₄   cup pesto (page 157)**
- **¹/₄   cup classic vinaigrette (page 92)**
- **1   T. balsamic vinegar**
- **1   T. sour cream**
- **¹/₄   t. pepper**
- **1   cup frozen green peas, thawed**

Pour over tortellini and toss. Serve hot or cold. Yield: 6 servings.

"To unmold, dip mold in warm but not hot water to the depth of the gelatin. Loosen around edge with a knife."

Seafoam Lime Mold

1 (3 oz.) pkg. lime Jello	**1²/₃ cups (13¹/₂ oz.) crushed**
1 cup boiling water	**pineapple, drained**
¹/₂ cup cold water	**¹/₂ cup chopped nuts**
1 T. lemon juice	**1 (8 oz.) pkg. cream cheese**
1¹/₂ cups miniature marshmallows	

Dissolve Jello in boiling water. Add cold water and lemon juice. Gradually add liquid mixture to softened cream cheese. Mix until well blended. Chill until almost firm. Fold in marshmallows, pineapple, and nuts. Pour into 1 quart mold. Chill until firm. Yield: 6 servings.

Seafood Mold

1½ cups water	2 T. prepared horseradish
½ lb. medium shrimp	2 T. lemon juice
1 cup mayonnaise	⅛ t. salt
½ cup flaked crabmeat	⅛ t. pepper
½ cup diced celery	1 envelope unflavored gelatin
2 T. diced onion	¼ cup water

Bring 1½ cups water to a boil in a saucepan; add shrimp. Cover and remove from heat. Let stand for 3 minutes. Drain well; rinse in ice cold water. Peel, devein, and chop shrimp finely.

Combine shrimp and next 8 ingredients; mix well, set aside.

Combine gelatin and ¼ cup water in a saucepan; let stand 5 minutes. Place saucepan over low heat, stirring until gelatin dissolves. Pour gelatin mixture into shrimp mixture; stir well. Pour mixture into a greased 3 cup mold. Chill until firm. Unmold and add garnishes of pimento, lemon slices, carrot curls, and fresh parsley, if desired. Yield: 6-8 servings.

Spinach Salad

1 bag fresh spinach, washed, drained and torn into pieces	½ cup bean sprouts
	¼ lb. bacon, cooked and crumbled
1 cup water chestnuts,	½ onion, sliced
1 cup fresh mushrooms, sliced	

Dressing:

¼ cup sugar	½ t. salt
⅛ cup vinegar	¼ cup salad oil
⅛ t. garlic salt	¼ cup ketchup

Combine first 6 ingredients. Mix together next 6 ingredients. Sprinkle with paprika, stir, and serve dressing with pitcher and spoon. Yield: 6-8 servings.

Taco Salad

1	lb. ground beef, browned with salt to taste, drained
$^1/_2$	head shredded lettuce
$^1/_2$	cup chopped onion
1	tomato, chopped
1	(15 oz.) can kidney beans, drained
$^1/_2$	lb. shredded longhorn cheese
	avocado slices
	ripe olives
1	(8 oz.) pkg. tortilla chips, crumbled

Combine the above ingredients. Toss with **Good Seasons Italian Dressing**. Yield: 6-8 servings.

"Season cottage cheese with fresh ginger, or freshly ground pepper."
"Fresh herbs are only half as potent as dried herbs, use twice the amount."

Tangy Romaine Salad

1	(10 oz.) pkg. fresh spinach or romaine lettuce
1	(12 oz.) pkg. small curd cottage cheese
$^1/_2$	cup chopped pecans
$^1/_2$	cup sour cream
$^1/_4$	cup sugar
2	T. horseradish
$^1/_2$	t. dry mustard
$^1/_4$	t. salt

Mix the first 3 ingredients together. Blend remaining ingredients in a mixer or a blender. Add the dressing to the spinach or lettuce and toss. Yield: 6 servings.

Tropical Lobster Salad

2 lb. lobster meat, cooked and cut in chunks	1 bunch watercress, stemmed and chopped
2 cups ripe papaya cubes	2 kiwi, peeled and cubed
3 scallions, chopped	

Dressing:

$^1/_2$ cup olive oil	$^1/_2$ t. tarragon
2 t. sour cream	$^1/_3$ t. Dijon mustard
$^1/_2$ T. white wine vinegar	salt and pepper to taste

Combine dressing ingredients and marinate lobster in it overnight. Just before serving, gently toss in papaya, kiwi, watercress, and scallions. Yield: 6 servings.

Vegetable Salad

1 head cauliflower	$^1/_4$ t. dried tarragon
3 medium zucchini	$^1/_2$ t. pepper
4 scallions	1 t. salt
$^1/_2$ pint cherry tomatoes	1 T. white wine vinegar
3 garlic cloves (large)	$^1/_3$ cup olive oil
1 t. Dijon mustard	1 head romaine lettuce

Break cauliflower into bite-sized flowerets and cook in boiling salted water for 4 minutes. Drain and put into a large bowl. Cut zucchini in half length-wise and across in $1^1/_2$ inch thick slices. Cook in boiling water 3 minutes. Add to cauliflower. Cut scallions into thin rounds and cut tomatoes in half and add to vegetables.

In food processor, chop garlic with steel blade. Add the mustard, seasonings, and vinegar. With the machine running, add oil through the feed tube. Pour dressing over vegetables and refrigerate until $^1/_2$ hour before serving. Line a salad bowl with romaine; toss vegetables again and season if necessary. Add to bowl. Yield: 8-10 servings.

Wild Rice and Turkey Salad

1	pkg. long grain wild rice, cooked and cooled	$^1/_2$	t. crumbled sage
			salt and pepper to taste
12	oz. broccoli flowerets		Grated zest and juice
$^1/_2$	cup oil		of one orange
2	T. balsamic vinegar	3	oz. coarsely chopped nuts
2	t. summer savory	2	cups turkey, cooked

Steam broccoli 5 minutes (cooked but crisp), drain and cool.

Whisk $^1/_2$ cup oil into vinegar. Add savory, sage, salt, and pepper. Mix in orange zest and juice. Add nuts.

Combine rice, broccoli, and dressing. Mix and toss well. Add turkey which has been cubed if desired. Chill. Yield: 6 servings.

USS Batfish

81

notes

Salad Dressings & Sauces

The crew of the Ingraham (DD-444) assembled before the commissioning in June 1941. Less than a year later, the ship sank in a collision with a tanker. Eleven crew members survived.

Salad Dressings & Sauces

Artichoke Salad Dressing

Bearnaise and Hollandaise Sauce

Bleu Cheese Dressing

Caesar Salad Dressing I and Croutons

Caesar Salad Dressing II

Caesar Salad Dressing III

Cocktail Sauce

Herbed Buttermilk Dressing

Lo-Cal Salad Dressing

No-Cal Salad Dressing

Papaya Seed Dressing

Peppercorn Dressing

Pesto Salad Dressing

Poppy Seed Dressing I

Poppy Seed Dressing II

Romaine Salad Dressing • Soubise Sauce

Sour Cream Dressing • Tartar Sauce

Thousand Island Dressing

Classic Vinaigrette • Pesto Vinaigrette

Tarragon Mustard Vinaigrette

Vinaigrette Dressing

Artichoke Salad Dressing

Cook one package **frozen artichoke hearts**. Drain.
Add to bottle of **Italian Salad Dressing** and refrigerate overnight.

Bearnaise and Hollandaise Sauce

Hollandaise Sauce:

  4 **egg yolks (room temperature)**
  $^3/_4$ **cup (1$^1/_2$ sticks) butter**
  4 **t. lemon juice (room temperature)**
      dash of each salt and cayenne

Put the egg yolks and lemon juice into a blender. Melt butter. Turn blender on low and beat the yolks for about 10 seconds. Slowly add the melted butter in a steady stream. Turn blender off. Yield: 1$^1/_2$ cups.

Bearnaise Sauce: To the Hollandaise sauce recipe, add **1 T. tarragon vinegar** and **1 t. each parsley, tarragon, and chervil** while the blender is on low speed. This stores easily in the refrigerator. Reheat on low in a double boiler. (If it gets too hot it will separate.)

Bleu Cheese Dressing

1 **cup mayonnaise**	**8** **oz. bleu cheese**
$^1/_2$ **cup buttermilk**	**1** **small clove garlic, pressed**

Blend mayonnaise and buttermilk together in a food processor. Add half bleu cheese and mix. Add garlic and dash of pepper. Crumble remainder of bleu cheese, and add to mixture. Refrigerate overnight. It will thicken. Dressing will last at least 2 months in refrigerator. Yield: 2 cups.

Caesar Salad Dressing I and Croutons

$^1/_2$ of a 2 oz. can anchovy fillets, drained	1 T. Dijon mustard
2 T. lemon juice	2 T. Parmesan cheese
	$^1/_4$ t. pepper

Beating mixture constantly with a wire whisk slowly pour $^1/_3$ **cup olive oil** in a thin steady stream until thicken. Yield: $^1/_2$ cup

Pour over one large head of **romaine lettuce** pieces. Sprinkle $^3/_4$ **cup grated Parmesan cheese** on top. Add croutons.

Croutons:

Cut $^1/_2$ of an **8" long loaf seeded Italian Bread** into 1 inch cubes. In a 12" skillet on medium high sauté the bread cubes in **3 T. oil**. Add $^1/_4$ **t. salt and** $^1/_4$ **t. pepper**, stirring until bread cubes are golden.

"Measure oil first, then measure honey in the same cup. Honey will slide right out."

"Crumble leftover bacon and use it for garnishing salads and soups."

Caesar Salad Dressing II

Cook **one egg** in boiling water for one minute. Put into a blender on high speed until fluffy. Drizzle $^3/_4$ **cup olive oil** on high speed. Turn to low speed then add:

$^1/_4$ cup fresh lemon juice	$^1/_2$ t. freshly ground pepper
1 clove garlic, pressed	1 t. salt
1 t. dry mustard	$^1/_4$ cup grated Parmesan cheese
1 t. Worcestershire sauce	

Cover and refrigerate until ready to use. Yield: $1^1/_4$ cups.

Caesar Salad Dressing III

$^3/_4$ cup olive oil

$^1/_4$ cup fresh lemon juice

2 garlic cloves

1 t. Worcestershire sauce

$^1/_2$ cup Parmesan cheese, grated

Combine all ingredients in processor or blender till smooth. Season with salt and pepper. Can be prepared 1 day ahead and stored, covered in the refrigerator. Yield: $1^1/_2$ cups.

Cocktail Sauce

1 cup ketchup

$^1/_4$ cup horseradish

3 dashes Worcestershire Sauce

1 cup chili sauce

3 dashes Tabasco

2 T. lemon juice

Mix all ingredients well and serve with boiled shrimp, clams, oysters on the half shell, or crabmeat cocktail. Yield: $^3/_4$ quart.

Herbed Buttermilk Dressing

1 cup buttermilk

2 T. parsley flakes

2 T. minced dried onion

$^1/_4$ t. dry basil

1 cup mayonnaise

$^1/_4$ t. oregano

$^1/_4$ t. rosemary

$^1/_4$ t. savory leaves

1 clove garlic, minced or pressed

Combine all but mayonnaise and let stand 5 minutes. Then with a wire whip, beat in 1 cup mayonnaise. Season to taste with salt and pepper, then cover and chill. Yield: 2 cups.

Lo-Cal Salad Dressing

¹/₄ cup olive oil	1 clove of garlic, crushed
¹/₄ cup water	¹/₂ t. salt
¹/₄ cup wine vinegar	1 t. dried tarragon

Mix all the above and blend by shaking in a jar and letting stand for several hours before its first use. Always shake before using. Use different herbs for variety. For extra tang, add 1 t. of Dijon mustard. Yield: ³/₄ cup.

No-Cal Salad Dressing

¹/₂ cup wine vinegar	1 clove garlic, crushed
¹/₂ t. salt	or ¹/₄ t. garlic powder
1 T. parsley	¹/₄ cup water

Mix well. Use other herbs and vinegars for variety. Tarragon is one of the best herbs for salad dressings. If available, try fruit vinegars such as strawberry or raspberry. Yield: ³/₄ cup.

Papaya Seed Dressing

¹/₂ cup sugar	1 cup salad oil
¹/₂ t. salt	¹/₂ small onion, chopped
¹/₂ t. dry mustard	2 T. fresh papaya seed
¹/₂ cup wine or tarragon vinegar	

Blend in blender or food processor until seeds resemble coarse pepper. Yield: 1¹/₂ cups.

Peppercorn Dressing

³/₄ cup sour cream
¹/₄ cup mayonnaise
2 T. fresh lemon juice
3-4 t. coarsely cracked pepper
1 t. Worcestershire sauce

1 beef bouillon cube
   dissolved in 4 t. warm water
   salt to taste
   milk (optional)

Combine all except milk and blend. To thin the dressing, add milk. Refrigerate at least 3 hours before serving.

Serve over combination of romaine, sliced mushrooms, cherry tomatoes, alfalfa sprouts, crumbled bacon. Can use almost anything. Excellent as a vegetable dip. Yield: 1 cup.

Pesto Salad Dressing

³/₄ cup olive oil
¹/₂ cup vinegar
3 T. sugar

¹/₄ cup fresh Pesto (page 157)
2 T. diced pimento

Combine all ingredients in an electric blender or food processor. Process at low speed until blended. Serve over salad greens. Yield: 1³/₄ cups.

Poppy Seed Dressing I

¹/₂ cup sugar
3 T. lemon juice
1 t. dry mustard
¹/₄ t. salt
¹/₃ cup honey

6 T. tarragon vinegar
1 cup applesauce
1 t. onion, grated
1 t. paprika
2 t. poppy seeds

In a blender, combine first 9 ingredients. Add poppy seeds. Serve on lettuce salad. Yield: 1¹/₂ cups.

Poppy Seed Dressing II

³/₄	cup sugar	1	onion, cut in quarters
1	t. dry mustard	1	cup oil
1	t. salt	1¹/₂	T. poppy seeds
¹/₃	cup vinegar		

Combine first five ingredients in blender until smooth. While blender is running, slowly add oil. Blend until thick. Add poppy seed. Great as a dressing for fresh fruit or on tossed salad. Yield: 1¹/₂ cups.

Romaine Salad Dressing

4	T. red wine vinegar	¹/₄	t. dry mustard
¹/₄	cup oil	¹/₄	t. salt
¹/₂	t. sugar	2	T. chopped parsley
1	egg yolk		

Mix together and pour over romaine lettuce. Yield: 6 servings.

Soubise Sauce

In the top of a double boiler: Melt **2 T. butter** and add **2 T. flour**.

When blended add: **2 cups chicken, fish, or veal stock**. Stir over low heat until thickened. Add **¹/₄ cup mushroom peelings**. Simmer about one hour. Strain and add dash of **nutmeg, salt, and pepper**.

Sauté: **2 medium onions, chopped** in **2 T. butter**.

Add to sauce and simmer over low heat for 30 minutes. Rub sauce through a fine sieve and add **2 T. whipping cream**. Yield: 2 cups.

"To peel oranges and grapefruit without the white membranes, soak fruit in hot water for several minutes before peeling."

Sour Cream Dressing

1 **cup sour cream**	1 **T. chopped chives**
6 **T. mayonnaise**	1 **t. celery seed**
1 **t. paprika**	1 **t. Worcestershire Sauce**
³/₄ **t. salt**	

Mix all ingredients and chill. Use on cabbage-pineapple salad, heads of lettuce, cold asparagus spears, cold beets, cold artichoke hearts, or tossed greens that include spinach. Yield: 1¹/₄ cups.

Tartar Sauce

1 **cup mayonnaise**	1 **t. grated onion**
1 **T. minced dill pickle**	1 **t. minced parsley**

Combine all ingredients. Chill. Yield: 1 cup.

Thousand Island Dressing

1 **cup mayonnaise**
¹/₂ **cup chili sauce**
1 **t. lemon juice**
1 **t. sugar**
¹/₂ **t. Worcestershire sauce**

Mix together. Store in refrigerator. Yield: 1¹/₂ cups.

"To crisp lettuce, celery, or carrots, soak briefly in cold water, wrap in paper towel, place in a plastic bag, and refrigerate for an hour."

Classic Vinaigrette

2	medium cloves garlic, minced	3	T. lemon juice
1¹/₂	cups olive oil	2	t. Dijon mustard
¹/₃	cup red wine vinegar	1	t. salt
¹/₄	cup finely chopped parsley	¹/₂	t. pepper

Combine ingredients in a blender and store, covered in refrigerator. Yield: 2 cups.
Use in Pesto Tortellini Salad (page 77).

Pesto Vinaigrette

¹/₈	t. minced garlic	1	t. fresh lemon juice
¹/₂	t. salt	2	T. tarragon vinegar
¹/₄	t. white pepper	¹/₂	cup olive oil
1	t. Dijon mustard	1	T. pesto (page 157)

Combine ingredients and serve over pasta salads. Yield: ³/₄ cup.

Tarragon Mustard Vinaigrette

²/₃	cup olive oil	³/₄	t. ground black pepper
¹/₂	T. Dijon mustard	1	t. salt
3	T. red wine vinegar	¹/₈	t. tarragon, crumbled

Combine ingredients. Will keep for several days refrigerated. Yield: ²/₃ cup.

Vinaigrette Dressing

²/₃	cup olive oil	1	garlic, crushed
¹/₃	cup red wine vinegar		pepper to taste
	dash of salt	1	t. prepared mustard

Combine ingredients, blending well. Serve on green salads. Yield: 1 cup.

Vegetables

USS Fearless MSO-442

Vegetables

Asparagus with Caper Dill Sauce
Broccoli Casserole
Broccoli with Fresh Mushrooms
Cabbage au Gratin
Carrots and Tarragon • Cauliflower-Carrot Pie
Egg Foo Yung • Easy Baked Beans
Fried Eggplant • Fried Green Tomatoes
Fried Rice • Frijoles • Funny Crab Cakes
Garden Potato Cups • Garlic Potatoes
Gourmet Potatoes
Marinated Vegetables • Mashed Potatoes
Mashed Potatoes with Cheddar Cheese and Cabbage
Nutted Wild Rice • Oven-Fried Potatoes
Perfect Boston Baked Beans — Crockpot Style
Potato Casserole • Potato Patties
Potato Scallop • Real "Chinese Rice"
Red Potatoes — Mashed • Southern Grits
Spinach Cheese Pie • Spinach Quiche
Spinach Supreme • Thelma's Squash Casserole
Tropical Glazed Sweet Potatoes
Twice-Baked Potatoes
Zucchini Parmesan I • Zucchini Parmesan II

Asparagus with Caper Dill Sauce

- 1 cup sour cream
- $^1/_4$ cup fresh lemon juice
- $^1/_4$ cup fresh dill (1 T. dried)
- $^1/_2$ cup capers, drained
- $^1/_2$ t. salt
- $^1/_2$ t. freshly ground black pepper
- 1 lb. fresh asparagus or green beans, blanched

Blend all ingredients except asparagus and chill for at least 1 hour. Serve over blanched asparagus. Yield: 4 servings.

Broccoli Casserole

- 2 pkgs. frozen chopped broccoli, cooked and well drained
- 2 eggs
- 1 can cream of mushroom soup
- 1 cup mayonnaise
- 1 onion, chopped
- 1 cup grated sharp cheese

Beat eggs and add other ingredients while broccoli is cooking. Stir in broccoli and turn into quart casserole. Dot with butter and sprinkle with chopped nuts. Bake at 350° for 30 minutes. Yield: 6-8 servings.

Broccoli with Fresh Mushrooms

2	T. salad oil	1	T. water
1	lb. fresh broccoli,	¹/₂	lb. fresh mushroms,
	cut in small flowerets,		cut in ¹/₄ inch slices
	with thick stems cut	2	green onions, finely chopped
	in ¹/₈ inch slices	¹/₄	t. ground nutmeg
1	t. sugar		dry roasted cashews (optional)
¹/₂	t. salt		

Place wok over high heat. When wok is hot, add 1 T. of the oil. When oil is hot, add broccoli, sugar, and salt; stir-fry for 1 minute. Add water, cover, and cook, stirring frequently, until broccoli is tender-crisp (about 3 minutes), adding more water, if needed; remove from wok and set aside.

Add remaining 1 T. oil. When oil is hot, add mushrooms, onions, and nutmeg; stir-fry until liquid evaporates (about 3 minutes). Return broccoli to wok and stir to heat through. Top with nuts, if you like. Yield: 4 servings.

Cabbage Au Gratin

1	medium cabbage,	¹/₄	cup milk
	coarsely shredded	¹/₂	t. salt
1	(10 oz.) can cream of	¹/₈	t. pepper
	celery soup, undiluted	¹/₂	cup fine, dry bread crumbs
1	cup (4 oz.) shredded	1	T. butter or margarine,
	American cheese		melted

Cook cabbage in boiling water 5-7 minutes until tender; drain well. Place cabbage in a lightly greased 1¹/₂ quart baking dish. Combine soup, milk, cheese, salt, and pepper; mix well. Pour over cabbage. Combine bread crumbs and butter, stirring well; sprinkle over cabbage. Bake at 350° for 15 minutes. Yield: 4 servings.

Carrots and Tarragon

1	lb. carrots, peeled and sliced		salt to taste
2	T. butter	2	t. tarragon leaves
1	t. sugar	1	T. chopped parsley

Cook carrots in water until tender crisp. Drain water and stir in remaining ingredients. Yield: 4 servings.

Cauliflower-Carrot Pie

3 cups herb-seasoned croutons, crushed

$^1/_4$ cup butter or margarine, melted

1 medium head cauliflower

$^1/_4$ cup butter or margarine

1 cup finely chopped onion

1 clove garlic, minced

$^1/_2$ cup thinly sliced carrots

$^1/_4$ t. salt

$^1/_4$ t. ground oregano

1 cup shredded Cheddar cheese, divided

2 eggs

$^1/_4$ cup milk

Combine first 2 ingredients; mix well. Press into a 9-inch pie plate; bake at 375° for 8 minutes. Set aside.

Remove outer leaves from cauliflower. Separate cauliflower into flowerets; wash thoroughly, and quarter flowerets.

Melt $^1/_4$ cup butter in a skillet; add cauliflower, onion, garlic, carrots, salt, and oregano. Cook over medium heat 10 minutes, stirring often.

Sprinkle $^1/_2$ cup cheese over crust. Spoon cooked vegetables into shell and top with remaining cheese. Combine eggs and milk; beat well and pour over pie. Bake at 375° for 35 minutes. Yield: 6-8 servings.

Egg Foo Yung

4 **eggs, beaten**	**$^1/_8$** **t. garlic powder**
$^1/_2$ **pound bean sprouts**	**$^1/_8$** **t. pepper**
$^1/_3$ **cup thinly sliced green onions**	**$^1/_2$** **t. salt**
$^1/_2$ **pound cooked crab,**	
small cooked shrimp,	
or slivered cooked chicken	

Foo Yung Sauce:

1 **t. cornstarch**	**1** **t. vinegar**
1 **t. sugar**	**$^1/_2$** **cup regular-strength**
2 **t. soy sauce**	**chicken broth**

Prepare Foo Yung sauce with above ingredients in wok over low heat. Stir until thickened (about 1 minute). Remove from wok. Keep warm.

Combine eggs, bean sprouts, onion, crab, garlic powder, pepper, and salt.

Place wok over medium-high heat. When wok is hot, add about 2 T. salad oil. When oil is hot, add $^1/_4$ cup of the egg mixture for each patty (make 2 or 3 at a time). Fry, turning once when lightly browned and cooked to your liking (about 2 minutes on each side). Continue with remaining batter until all patties are cooked, adding more oil as needed. Remove to warm platter and pour Foo Yung sauce over patties. Yield: 6 servings.

"If brown sugar has become hard, add a slice of bread
or apple and seal tightly."

"To remove a coconut from its shell put the whole coconut
into a preheated 425° oven for 10-15 minutes.
Let the coconut cool to touch."

Easy Baked Beans

2 (16 oz.) cans pork and beans
³/₄ cup brown sugar
¹/₂ cup ketchup
1 T. dry mustard
6 slices bacon cut into pieces

Empty one can beans into bottom of greased casserole. Combine sugar and mustard; sprinkle one-half of mixture over beans. Top with other can of beans. Sprinkle with remainder of sugar and mustard mixture, chopped bacon and ketchup over beans. Bake uncovered at 300° for 2 hours. Yield 6 servings.

Fried Eggplant

1 egg, beaten
¹/₂ cup milk
¹/₂ cup cornmeal
¹/₄ cup flour
1 t. salt
1 eggplant, sliced in ¹/₂ inch circles
¹/₂ cup oil

Combine egg and milk; set aside. Combine cornmeal, flour, and salt. Dip eggplant slices in egg mixture and then dredge in cornmeal mixture.

Heat oil in large skillet over medium-high heat. Arrange a single layer of eggplant in skillet; cook until golden brown on each side. Fork should pierce the eggplant easily when done. Repeat with remaining slices, adding additional oil if needed. Remove to a serving platter and top with a teaspoon of sour cream on each slice. Yield: 4-6 servings.

Fried Green Tomatoes

 1   **egg, beaten**
 ¹/₂   **cup milk**
 ¹/₂   **cup cornmeal**
 ¹/₄   **cup all-purpose flour**
 1   **t. salt**
 ¹/₂   **t. pepper**
 4   **medium size green tomatoes, cut into ¹/₃ inch slices**
 3-4   **T. vegetable oil**

Combine egg and milk; set aside. Combine cornmeal, flour, salt, and pepper. Dip tomatoes in egg mixture; dredge in cornmeal mixture.

Heat 3 T. oil in large skillet over medium heat. Arrange a single layer of tomato slices in skillet and cook until golden brown on each side. Remove to a serving platter and top with a teaspoon of sour cream. Yield: 6-8 servings.

Fried Rice

 1   **egg, beaten**
 2   **T. butter**
 2   **cups cooked rice**
 1   **cup chopped onion**
 ¹/₂   **cup diced cooked shrimp or bacon**
 ¹/₄   **lb. fresh mushrooms, sliced and sautéed**
 2   **T. soy sauce**

Heat butter in skillet and scramble egg quickly in pan. Add onion and cook 1 minute. Add remaining ingredients except soy sauce. Cook 5 minutes, stirring gently. Add soy sauce and stir. Cook 2 minutes longer. Serve immediately or put in covered casserole and keep warm in low oven. Yield: 4 servings.

Frijoles (El Paso-style Pinto Beans)

1   **cup dry pinto beans**
5   **cups water**
1   **ham hock**
¹/₂ **cup diced salt pork**
1   **small onion, sliced**
1   **clove garlic, minced**
1   **t. sugar**
1   **t. chili powder**
    salt

Cover beans with cold water and soak overnight. Drain; rinse with cold running water.

Heat beans, 5 cups water, the ham hock, salt pork, onion, garlic, sugar, and chili powder in Dutch oven to boiling; reduce heat. Simmer until beans are tender, about 2 hours. Salt to taste. Yield: 6-8 servings.

Funny Crab Cakes

3   **cups grated zucchini**
2   **eggs**
1   **cup seasoned bread crumbs**
1   **T. mayonnaise**
2   **T. grated onion**
1   **t. Old Bay seasoning**
2-4 **T. flour, if needed to make patties**

Combine all ingredients. Drop by tablespoon in a little oil and cook slowly. Turn once and cook till done. Serve with cocktail sauce. If you peel the zucchini before grating, it will "look" like real crab cakes! Yield: 4-6 servings.

Garden Potato Cups

4   **medium baking potatoes**
¹/₄   **cup butter or margarine**
1   **small onion, chopped**
2   **cups shredded cabbage**
1   **cup grated carrots**
¹/₂   **cup water**
¹/₃   **cup chopped green pepper**
¹/₂   **t. salt**
¹/₈   **t. white pepper**

Wash potatoes and bake at 400° for 1 hour or until done.

Melt butter in a large skillet or wok, add onion and sauté until tender. Add cabbage, carrots and water; cover and simmer for 10 minutes. Stir in green pepper. Cook, uncovered, an additional 5 minutes or until liquid is absorbed.

Cut cooked potatoes in half lengthwise; carefully scoop out pulp, leaving ¹/₄ inch shell. Mash pulp.

Combine cabbage mixture and mashed potato pulp mixing well. Stir in salt and pepper. Stuff shells with potato mixture. Bake at 400° for 15 minutes. Yield: 8 servings.

Garlic Potatoes

1   **lb. small new potatoes (about 10), scrubbed**
6   **large cloves garlic, peeled and smashed**
3   **T. olive oil**
³/₄   **t. salt**

Place potatoes in a 1¹/₂ quart souffle dish. Add remaining ingredients and stir to coat potatoes. Cover tightly and cook in a microwave on **HIGH** for 10-15 minutes.

Remove from oven. Uncover and serve hot. Yield: 4-6 servings.

Gourmet Potatoes

6	large potatoes	1	cup sour cream
1/4	cup butter, melted	1	t. salt
1/3	cup onion, chopped	1/4	t. pepper
1-2	cups Cheddar cheese, shredded		paprika

Cook potatoes in skins. Cool, peel, and shred coarsely. In a saucepan, sauté onion in butter. Do not brown. Fold potatoes, onion, cheese, and sour cream together. Add salt and pepper. Place in greased casserole dish, sprinkle with paprika, and bake at 350° for 25 minutes. May be made ahead of time and frozen. Yield: 8 servings.

Marinated Vegetables

2	cups cauliflower flowerets	1	medium zucchini, sliced
2	cups sliced carrots	1	medium cucumber,
1 1/2	cups broccoli flowerets		cut in half lenthwise and sliced
1 1/2	cups sliced fresh mushrooms	2/3	cup diced green pepper
3	stalks celery, diagonally sliced		Dressing (recipe follows)

Combine first 8 ingredients in a large bowl. Pour dressing over vegetables, and toss gently. Cover and chill at least 12 hours. Yield: 10 servings.

Dressing

3/4	cup tarragon vinegar	1/2	t. dried whole tarragon
1/4	cup olive oil	1/4	t. prepared mustard
2	T. vegetable oil	1/4	t. salt
2	T. sugar	1/4	t. pepper
1	large clove garlic, crushed		

Combine all ingredients, mixing well. Yield: 1 1/4 cups.

Mashed Potatoes

4 cups hot mashed potatoes

1 cup sour cream

¹/₃ cup sharp Cheddar cheese, cubed

¹/₂ t. salt

Mix together; bake in a greased casserole at 350° for 15 minutes. Yield: 4-6 servings.

"To whiten boiled potatoes, squeeze a few drops of lemon in the water."

"To prevent discoloration when grating raw potatoes, grate directly into a bowl of ice water."

Mashed Potatoes
with Cheddar Cheese and Cabbage

¹/₂ large green cabbage, thinly sliced (8 cups)

2¹/₂ lb. russet potatoes, peeled and chopped

¹/₂ cup unsalted butter, cut into pieces

¹/₄ cup green onion tops, chopped

1 cup Cheddar cheese, grated

Cook cabbage in boiling salted water until tender, about 2 minutes. Transfer to bowl, drain. Return water in pot to boil. Add potatoes and cook until tender, about 20 minutes. Drain and add butter. Beat with an electric mixer until mashed. Mix in onion tops and cabbage. Spoon potato mixture into an 8 cup greased baking dish. Sprinkle with cheese. Bake in a 350° oven until heated thorough, about 30 minutes. Yield: 8-10 servings.

Spinach Cheese Pie

1	pie crust
1	(10 oz.) pkg. frozen chopped spinach
6	eggs
1	(3 oz.) pkg. cream cheese, softened
$^1/_4$	cup shredded sharp process American cheese
2	t. sliced green onion
1	T. snipped parsley
$^1/_2$	t. salt
	dash pepper
2	T. grated Parmesan cheese

Cook spinach according to package directions, drain well. Combine eggs, cream cheese, and shredded cheese; beat until well blended. Stir in spinach, green onions, parsley, salt, and pepper. Turn into baked pie shell and top with Parmesan cheese. Bake in 425° oven for 15 minutes or until edges of filling are set. Remove from oven and let stand 10 minutes before serving. Yield: 6-8 servings.

Spinach Quiche

1	9 inch unbaked pie shell	$1^1/_4$	cups half and half
1	cup grated Swiss cheese	3	eggs
1	(10 oz.) pkg. frozen, chopped spinach, cooked and drained	1	t. salt
		2	T. butter

Preheat oven to 450°. Bake quiche pastry for 5 minutes. Set aside. Reduce oven to 375°. Spread $^3/_4$ of the cheese and spinach on bottom of pastry. Beat cream, egg, and salt together until frothy. Pour over cheese and spinach. Sprinkle with remaining cheese and dot with butter. Bake for 25-30 minutes or until filling is set. Yield: 6-8 servings.

Spinach Supreme

3	pkgs. (10 oz.) frozen chopped spinach	1	t. dry mustard
4	T. butter		dash cayenne
3	T. flour	1	cup milk
$^1/_2$	t. salt	$^3/_4$	cup grated Parmesan cheese
$1^1/_2$	t. spicy mustard	4	T. cream
		$^1/_2$	cup grated Swiss cheese

Cook spinach and drain well. Set aside. Melt butter in saucepan and add flour and seasonings. Blend in milk and cook a little. Add cheeses, reserving $^1/_4$ cup Parmesan for topping. Cook creamed mixture for 5 minutes, then add spinach. Pour into buttered casserole dish and refrigerate or freeze until ready to use. Bake in 350° oven for 30 minutes. Yield: 6 servings.

"Vegetables grown above the ground should be started in boiling water and vegetables grown below the ground should be started in cold water."

Thelma's Squash Casserole

2   cups cooked squash
2   slices white bread soaked in 1 cup milk
$^1/_2$ cup onion
2   cups grated cheddar cheese (use one cup in squash and one on top)
2   eggs, beaten

Combine the above ingredients and put in a greased casserole dish. Brown enough bread crumbs in margarine and sprinkle on top of the casserole along with the 1 cup cheese and bake in a 350° oven for 30 minutes. Yield: 4-6 servings.

Tropical Glazed Sweet Potatoes

4	large sweet potatoes	¹/₈	t. ground cinnamon
1	(8 oz.) can crushed pineapple, undrained	2	t. grated orange rind
³/₄	cup firmly packed brown sugar	1	cup canned apricots, undrained and puréed
1¹/₂	T. cornstarch	2	T. butter or margarine, softened
¹/₄	t. salt	¹/₂	cup chopped pecans

Cook sweet potatoes in boiling water 20-25 minutes or until tender. Let cool to touch; peel and cut into ¹/₂ inch slices. Arrange slices so edges overlap in a lightly greased 12 x 8 x 2 inch baking dish; set aside.

Drain pineapple, reserving ¹/₃ cup syrup; set pineapple aside. Combine pineapple syrup, sugar, cornstarch, salt, cinnamon, orange rind, and apricot purée in a heavy saucepan; stir well. Cook over medium heat, stirring constantly, until smooth and thickened. Add butter, pecans, and pineapple, stirring until butter melts; pour mixture over potatoes. Bake at 375° for 20-25 minutes. Yield: 8 servings.

Twice-Baked Potatoes

2	medium baking potatoes	¹/₄	t. salt
¹/₂	cup cream-style cottage cheeese	¹/₈	t. pepper
2	T. butter, softened	1	T. chopped chives
1	T. mayonnaise	3	T. shredded cheddar cheese

Wash potatoes thoroughly and rub skins with oil. Bake for 1 hour in a 400° oven until done.

After potatoes are cool cut them in half lengthwise and scoop out the pulp. Set the skin/shells aside. Mash pulp and add the next 6 ingredients, mixing well. Stuff shells with potato mixture; sprinkle with cheese. Place in a shallow baking dish, cover with foil, and heat until warm in a 350° oven for 10-15 minutes. Yield: 4 servings.

Zucchini Parmesan I

4-5 **zucchini squash, sliced (about 3 cups)**

2 **T. butter or margarine**

¹/₂ **t. salt**

2 **T. grated Parmesan cheese**

Sauté zucchini in melted butter in a wok. Add salt. Turn off heat and cover for about 10 minutes. Sprinkle with cheese, toss and serve. Yield: 8 servings.

Zucchini Parmesan II

4 **medium zucchini**

3 **T. butter**

2 **T. sour cream**

2 **T. Parmesan cheese, grated**

Shred zucchini in food processor. Melt butter in skillet; add zucchini, sour cream, and cheese. Sauté for about 5 minutes. Yield: 6 servings.

"Season carrots with thyme, honey, or mint.
ason peas with thyme, basil, mint, or onion.
Season cooked green beans with bacon or
chicken broth, summer savory or
sesame oil and soy sauce.
Season cooked potatoes with
cheese, onion, or dill."

Entrees

Luncheon for the Staff

Seafood

Bagwell's Opakapaka

Baked Whole Salmon Seattle Style

Boiled Shrimp

Chinese Scallops in Oyster Sauce

Crab Cakes • Crab Casserole

Creamed Scallops

Fish Cakes

Haddock Casserole

Hot Crab Souffle

Hot and Sour Shrimp Stir-Fry

Lutefish

Maryland Crab Cakes

Quiche with Crab

Salmon Fillets on the Barbecue Grill

Salmon with Champagne Cream Sauce

Sauteed Oysters with Basil

Scallop and Shrimp Sauce

Shrimp Creole

Shrimp Thermidor

Stir-Fry Shrimp

Vegetable and Scallop Stir-Fry

Bagwell's Opakapaka

Snapper (blue, red, or grey) Sole or Mahi-Mahi (3 oz. per serving)

Heat 2 Tablespoons of oil and 2 Tablespoons of butter in a skillet; flour, salt, and pepper fish and sauté 10 minutes. Remove to glass dish and cover with foil and put in a low warm oven to keep warm until sauce is made.

Sauce:
- $^1/_2$ **cup white wine**
- 2-3 **T. minced shallots**
- 2-3 **bay leaves**
- 1 **T. whole peppercorns**

Mix and reduce this amount by half over medium heat in the same pan you sautéed the fish. Once reduced, add **1 cup cream** and **2-3 T. butter**, **2 pinches of fresh grated ginger** and **juice of half a lemon**. Yield: $1^1/_2$ cups.

Put fish on watercress, sprinkle with ginger and pour sauce on top.

Baked Whole Salmon Seattle Style

Whole salmon,	**paprika**
head and tail removed	$^1/_2$ **cup melted butter**
4 **T. lemon juice**	**onion rings**
salt and pepper	

Place whole salmon in a foil lined pan. Bake in a 350° oven for 20 minutes, uncovered. Remove fish from oven and peel off the top skin and pour lemon juice over the exposed fish. Salt generously, add pepper and paprika. Pour melted butter over top and top with onion rings. Return to the oven and continue to bake uncovered for 1 hour. Serve with baked potatoes. Yield: allow $^1/_3$ lb. of fish per person.

115

Boiled Shrimp

2 lb. shrimp

Bring about 8 cups of water to a boil. Add shrimp. Remove from heat, cover. Leave for 3 minutes. Drain and put shrimp in ice water for 5 minutes. Drain and peel.

*"Season cooked fish with dill, onion, lemon,
celery, basil, or dry white wine."*

Chinese Scallops in Oyster Sauce

2 T. oyster sauce

2 t. cornstarch

1 t. soy sauce

¹/₄ t. sugar

¹/₂ lb. scallops, well rinsed, drained, and sliced across grain

2 T. butter or margarine

¹/₂ cup (3 oz.) snow peas

¹/₄ cup chopped green onion

Combine oyster sauce, cornstarch, soy, and sugar. Stir scallops into oyster sauce mixture; set aside.

Place wok over medium heat. When wok is hot, add butter. When butter has melted, add peas and onion and stir-fry for 2-3 minutes or until vegetables are tender-crisp. Raise heat to high, add scallop mixture, and stir-fry for about 3 minutes or until scallops are just opaque throughout and sauce is slightly thickened. Spoon over hot cooked rice and serve immediately. Yield: 4 servings.

Crab Cakes

2 thin slices of bread, crust removed and diced fine	dash of paprika
	dash of nutmeg
1/2 cup mayonnaise	1/2 t. Worcestershire sauce
1 large egg, separated	1 T. parsley, minced
1/4 t. salt	1 lb. cooked fresh crabmeat

In a medium mixing bowl, mix bread and mayonnaise and let stand about 5 minutes. Add unbeaten egg yolk, seasonings, and crab. With a fork, mix lightly but well.

Beat egg white until stiff. Fold into crab mixture.

Shape the mixture into about 12 cakes using about 1/4 cup of the crab mixture for each.

Brush a large skillet with butter and add the cakes. Over medium heat brown on both sides for about 10 minutes. Yield: 4-6 servings.

"To eliminate lingering fish odors from the kitchen, boil a small amount of vinegar."

Crab Casserole

1 pound crabmeat	2 T. mustard
1 stick butter (softened)	2 T. Worcestershire sauce
1 cup bread crumbs	salt and pepper
2 T. mayonnaise	

Mix all ingredients together. Put in casserole dish. Bake 45 minutes at 350°. Serve hot. Yield: 4-6 servings.

Creamed Scallops

1	lb. scallops	¹/₂	lb. mushrooms, sliced
¹/₂	cup dry white wine		salt to taste
2	T. butter		bread crumbs
2	T. flour		Parmesan cheese
²/₃	cup light cream or milk		butter
2	t. lemon juice		

Drain scallops, reserving liquid. Cook scallops in wine for 5 minutes. Drain and reserve liquid. Make roux of melted butter, flour, and cream. Add liquid from scallops and stir until smooth and thick. Add scallops, lemon juice, mushrooms, and salt. Put in buttered ramekins or small casserole, and sprinkle with bread crumbs and cheese. Dot with butter. Bake at 400° until brown. Yield: 4 servings.

Fish Cakes

³/₄	cup salted cooked codfish	1	egg, well beaten
1	cup mashed potatoes	2	T. cream

Combine well. Shape into small flat cakes and sauté in butter on both sides. Yield: 4-6 servings.

118

Haddock Casserole

2	lbs. frozen haddock fillets	1	small onion, minced
1/4	cup butter or margarine	2	T. salad oil
4	T. flour	1	(10 oz.) pkg. frozen peas,
2	cups milk		cooked and drained
1	cup sharp Cheddar cheese,	1	cup sour cream
	grated		salt and pepper
1/2	lb. fresh mushrooms, sliced		

Barely cover haddock with water and simmer gently for 15 minutes, or until fish flakes with a fork; drain and flake meat in large chunks. While fish is cooking, melt butter; blend in flour. Add milk, and stirring, cook over low heat until smooth and thick. Add cheese and cook until it melts; remove sauce from heat.

Sauté mushrooms and onion in salad oil for 5 minutes; add to cream sauce, along with cooked peas, sour cream, and flaked fish. Mix lightly, add salt and pepper to taste, and turn into a shallow 3 quart casserole or baking dish. Heat under the broiler until bubbly and lightly browned on top. Yield: 8 servings.

Hot Crab Souffle

8	slices white bread	3	cups milk
2	cups crab or shrimp	4	eggs
1/2	cup mayonnaise	1	can mushroom soup
1	onion, chopped		grated cheese
1	cup celery		paprika
1	green pepper, chopped		

Dice half of bread into baking dish. Mix crab, mayonnaise, onion, pepper, celery, and spoon over bread. Trim crusts from remaining 4 slices and place over crab mixture.

Mix eggs and milk and pour over mixture. Place in refrigerator overnight.

Bake in a 325° for 15 minutes. Remove from oven and spoon mushroom soup over top. Top with cheese, sprinkle with paprika, and bake one hour at 325°. Yield: 8-10 servings.

Hot and Sour Shrimp Stir-Fry

1 lb. medium size fresh unpeeled shrimp	1 cup fresh sliced mushrooms
2 T. soy sauce	1 T. vegetable oil
2 T. rice vinegar	4 green onions, halved lengthwise and cut into 2 inch pieces
1 t. sugar	2 cups fresh snow peas, halved diagonally
¼ t. crushed red pepper	4 cups hot cooked rice
2 cloves garlic minced	

Peel and devein shrimp. Combine shrimp and next 5 ingredients in a shallow bowl; stir well. Cover and marinate in refrigerator 30 minutes, stirring occasionally.

Heat wok to medium-high. Add oil, green onions; stir-fry 1 minute. Add mushrooms; stir-fry 2 minutes. Add snow peas; stir-fry 1 minute. Add shrimp mixture; stir-fry 2 minutes or until shrimp turns pink. Serve over rice. Yield: 4-6 servings.

Lutefish

1 lb. box salted cod

Use stainless steel or teflon for soaking and cooking. Soak in water around 5 pm the night before serving to wash off salt. Soak until 11 pm. Change water and soak overnight.

8 am: Drain and change water.

Into an 8 oz. glass add 6 T. baking soda. Fill glass with water and stir to mix. Add soda water to fish and stir to blend.

At supper time (5 pm) drain soda water and replace with fresh water to cover fish.

Cook over stove. Let water come to almost a boil and cook uncovered on simmer for 15 minutes. Drain and place fish in serving bowl or platter.

Serve with melted butter and boiled potatoes. Yield: 4-6 servings.

Maryland Crab Cakes

1	cup breadcrumbs	1	T. Worcestershire sauce
2	eggs, beaten	2	T. fresh parsley, finely chopped
1/2	t. white pepper	2/3	cup mayonnaise
2	t. salt	1	lb. crab meat
2	t. prepared mustard		

Mix together gently and form into 1 dozen cakes. Deep fry at 350° about 3-5 minutes each side until golden brown. Serve with Tartar Sauce, (page 91). Yield: 1 dozen.

Quiche with Crab

1	unbaked pastry shell	1²/₃	cups crabmeat
1/2	cup mayonnaise	1	(8 oz.) pkg. Swiss cheese,
2	T. flour		shredded
2	eggs, beaten	1/3	cup green onions
1/2	cup milk or half and half		

Bake pastry shell for 5 minutes in a 350° oven. Remove and set aside.

Mix mayonnaise, flour, eggs, and milk together. Stir in crabmeat, cheese, and onions. Pour into shell and bake 40-45 minutes at 350°. Yield: 6-8 servings.

Salmon Fillets on the Barbecue Grill

Fillet a **whole salmon**. Take the back bone out. The fish is now in two halfs. Take out the side bones with a tweezer. Cut into serving pieces — about 6 oz. each. Lay the cut pieces on a foil lined cookie sheet. Melt **1 cup butter** and **2 T. lemon juice** and pour over the salmon and be sure to get some of the mixture under the skin. **Salt and pepper** and cook about 20-25 minutes over direct heat on the Weber grill. Do not cover the fish. Yield: allow 1/3 lb. fish per person.

Salmon with Champagne Cream Sauce

2   T. ($^1/_4$ stick) butter
$^1/_4$ cup chopped shallots
2   cups dry Champagne
    or sparkling white wine

2   cups whipping cream
6   (8 oz.) salmon fillets,
    $^3/_4$ inch thick

Melt butter in skillet over medium heat. Add shallots and sauté 3 minutes. Increase heat to high. Add Champagne and boil until liquid is reduced to $^1/_2$ cup, about 15 minutes. Add cream and boil until thickened to sauce consistency, stirring occasionally, about 10 minutes. Season to taste with salt and pepper. Set aside. This can be prepared one day in advance. Cover and refrigerate.

Bake salmon fillets at 400° for 20 minutes. Remove from oven, put fillet on a plate and top with 2-4 tablespoons of the Champagne Cream Sauce. Yield: 6 servings.

Sautéed Oysters with Basil

1   pint Pacific oysters
2   T. butter or margarine

$^1/_2$ t. dry basil
2   T. dry white wine

Rinse and gently pat oysters dry. Dredge in 2 T. flour and shake off excess.

Place wok over medium-high heat. When wok is hot, add butter. When butter has melted, add oysters and sprinkle with basil. Stir-fry oysters gently for about 4 minutes. Arrange on a serving dish and keep warm.

Add wine to wok and stir up browned particles. Spoon liquid over oysters. Yield: 2 servings.

Scallop and Shrimp Sauce

Sauté a **small chopped onion** and a **few dried green tomatoes** in **butter**. Add **2 cups cream** and simmer for 10 minutes.

Stir-fry **2 cups scallops** and **2 cups medium shrimp** in **2 T. butter** and **2 T. oil** until opaque and add to sauce.

Cook **one pound fettucini**. Pour sauce over the pasta. Yield: 6-8 servings.

Shrimp Creole

1	cup chopped onion	1	cup water
1	cup chopped celery	1	t. Worcestershire sauce
1	cup chopped green pepper	1	bay leaf
1	clove garlic (minced)	1	t. salt
4	T. butter or shortening		Dash of Tabasco sauce
2	cups canned tomatoes		or cayenne pepper
$^1/_2$	(6 oz.) can tomato paste	1	lb. shrimp

In skillet, sauté onion, celery, green pepper, and garlic in butter for 5-10 minutes. Add remaining ingredients except shrimp and simmer for 45 minutes. Add shrimp and simmer another 10 minutes. Serve over rice. Remove bay leaf before serving. Yield: 4 servings.

Shrimp Thermidor

$^1/_2$	cup fresh mushrooms, sliced	$^1/_2$	t. dry mustard
$^1/_4$	cup butter, melted		dash cayenne
$^1/_4$	cup flour	2	cups milk
1	t. salt	$^3/_4$	lb. shrimp, cooked

Sauté the mushrooms in butter for 5 minutes. Add the next four ingredients and blend well. Add milk and cook, stirring constantly, until thickened.

Stir in cooked shrimp, peeled and deveined.

Transfer to 6 ramekins or $1^1/_2$ quart casserole. Sprinkle with grated fresh Parmesan cheese. Bake at 400° for 10 minutes. Yield: 6 servings.

123

Stir-Fry Shrimp

3 T. bacon lard	1/2 cup onion, finely chopped
2 cups shrimp, peeled & deveined	1/4 cup green pepper, finely chopped

Heat bacon lard in wok on medium-high. Sauté onion and green pepper for 2 minutes. Add shrimp and stir-fry about 2 minutes until cooked. Serve with Southern Grits (page 108) or rice. Yield: 2 servings.

Vegetable and Scallop Stir-Fry

3 T. soy sauce	3 green onions, sliced
1 t. cornstarch	1 carrot, sliced
2 T. sesame oil	1 zucchini, sliced
2 T. peanut oil	2 large garlic cloves, finely chopped
8 asparagus spears, cut into 1 inch pieces	2 t. fresh ginger, minced
6 mushrooms, sliced	1/2 lb. scallops

Mix soy sauce and cornstarch. Heat oils in wok over medium-high heat. Add vegetables, garlic, and ginger. Stir-fry for 3-4 minutes. Add scallops and stir-fry about 1 minute. Add soy sauce mixture to wok. Stir until it thickens and scallops are opaque. Yield: 4 servings.

Chicken

Carol's Curried Chicken

Cashew Chicken for Two

Chicken and Artichoke Casserole

Chicken and Mushrooms

Chicken and Stuffing

Chicken Casserole • Chicken Florentine

Chicken in Mushroom and Wine Sauce

Chicken Liver Stroganoff

Chicken or Fish Picante

Chicken Party Rolls

Chicken Scallopini • Chicken with Basil

Chicken with 40 Cloves Garlic

Chicken with Peppers and Pecans

Easy Chicken Casserole

Golden Chicken Nuggets

Honey Chicken

Kung Pao Chicken • Lemon Chicken

Mexican Chicken Breasts

Oven Fried Chicken with Herbs

Quesadillas • Shake and Bake

Slivered Chicken and Walnuts

Carol's Curried Chicken

2 chickens, boiled in salted water,
   boned into chunks. Save stock.
¹/₂ lb. butter
2 T. curry powder
¹/₂ t. ginger
   salt and pepper
3 T. sugar
1 medium onion, chopped
¹/₈ t. garlic powder
1 cup flour
1¹/₂ cups milk
1¹/₂ cups chicken stock
3 T. lemon juice
1 cup raisins
1 cup frozen peas
1 cup water chestnuts

Combine flour, curry powder, ginger, salt, pepper, and sugar. Set aside. Melt butter and sauté onion; add garlic powder. Add dry ingredients with milk and stock alternately until a thin sauce is made (approximately 3 cups of liquid). Add lemon juice and simmer one hour. Add raisins, peas, and water chestnuts to sauce. Add chicken meat. Serve over rice. Yield: 10-12 servings.

Condiments:

crumbled bacon	chutney
chopped peanuts	crushed pineapple
coconut	banana slices rolled in sugar
cucumber chips	

Cashew Chicken for Two

1	t. cornstarch
$1/2$	cup chicken broth
1	T. each cornstarch and soy sauce
1	lb. chicken breast, skinned, boned, and cut into small pieces
1	stalk of celery, thinly sliced
$1/4$	lb. green beans, cut in $1/2$ inch slanting slices
1	large carrot, cut in $1/4$ inch slanting slices
1	small onion, cut in half, then in $1/4$ inch slices
1	clove garlic, minced or pressed
4	T. oil
2	T. water
$1/3$	cup roasted cashews

Mix the 1 t. cornstarch with chicken broth; set aside. Combine the 1 T. cornstarch, soy, and chicken. Mix well to coat chicken thoroughly; set aside.

Place wok on high heat. When wok is hot, add 2 T. of oil. When oil is hot, add chicken mixture. Stir-fry until chicken is opaque (about 3 minutes); remove chicken from wok and set aside.

Add remaining 2 T. oil to wok. When oil is hot, add celery, beans, carrot, onion, and garlic. Stir-fry for 1 minute. Add water, cover, and cook for about 3 minutes or until vegetables are just tender-crisp.

Return chicken and chicken broth mixture to pan. Stir until liquid boils and thickens (about 1 minute). Stir in most of the cashews. Garnish with remaining cashews. Yield: 2 servings.

Chicken and Artichoke Casserole

Make **Bouquet Garni**:

  2 **sprigs parsley**

  1 **celery top**

  1 **carrot, peeled and chopped**

  1 **bay leaf**

  1 **t. diced thyme**

Place **2 cut-up broiler-fryers (3 lb.)** in 2 cups salted water with bouquet garni. Cook and simmer one hour till tender. Cool in stock. Remove meat in good sized pieces and arrange in casserole with **2 (10 oz.) pkgs. cooked artichoke hearts**.

Cheese Sauce:

  $^1\!/_4$ **cup butter**

  $^1\!/_4$ **cup flour**

  2 **cups chicken stock**

  3 **cups shredded mild Cheddar cheese**

  $^1\!/_2$ **t. nutmeg**

Melt butter, add flour. Stir in chicken stock. Cook, stirring, until thick. Stir in cheese and nutmeg. Pour over chicken and artichoke hearts.

Sprinkle with $^1\!/_2$ **cup fine dry breadcrumbs, 1 t. savory, 1 t. thyme,**. Slice **2 T. butter** over the crumbs.

Can refrigerate or freeze at this point.

Bake uncovered at 350° for 30 minutes or until golden brown. Yield: 8-10 servings.

"Learning to cut up a chicken is economical."
"One pound of fresh mushrooms sliced and cooked is the equivilent of one 8 ounce can of sliced mushrooms."

Chicken and Mushrooms

6	T. butter	2	cups sliced mushrooms
$^1/_4$	t. thyme	1	cup white wine
1	t. paprika	$1^1/_2$ - 2	lb. chicken pieces
1	t. salt		flour
$^1/_4$	t. pepper		

Melt butter in a baking dish. Stir in thyme, paprika, salt and pepper. Dredge chicken pieces in flour. Place meaty side down in butter mixture. Bake at 400° for 20 minutes. Reduce heat to 350 degrees and add the mushrooms and wine. Cover with foil and bake 40 minutes longer. Yield: 6 servings.

Chicken and Stuffing

5   whole chicken breasts, deboned, skinless
1   (8 oz.) pkg. Swiss cheese slices
2   (10$^3/_4$ oz.) cans cream of chicken soup
1   pkg. dry herb-seasoned stuffing mix
$^1/_2$ cup margarine, melted

Skin, bone and cut the chicken breasts in half. Arrange chicken in 9 x 13 inch pan. Place cheese on top of chicken. Spread undiluted soup over cheese. Toss melted margarine with stuffing mix and spread over soup. Bake uncovered, in 350° oven for 1 hour or until chicken is done. Yield: 5 servings.

"Never wash mushrooms — they will become watery. Just brush them with a paper towel or soft cloth to remove the sterile soil they are grown in."

Chicken Casserole

4	large chicken breasts,	1	cup fresh mushrooms, chopped
	split and skinned	2	t. mint leaves
	salt and pepper		(or bottled mint sauce)
	paprika	1	can cream of mushroom soup,
	lemon juice		undiluted
4	T. oil	1/3	cup Parmesan cheese
	flour		

Dry chicken breasts and sprinkle with salt, pepper, paprika, and lemon juice on both sides. Brown in oil. Sprinkle a little flour on top to aid browning. When brown, remove from skillet and place in a single layer in casserole. Brown mushrooms in same skillet and pour over chicken. Sprinkle mint leaves or sauce over all. Pour mushroom soup over the chicken and cover with Parmesan cheese. More cheese and mushrooms may be used if desired. Bake at 350° for 40 minutes. Yield: 4 servings.

Friday Night Sit-Down Dinner

Baked Potato Soup, page 35
Cottage Cheese Buns, page 52
Spinach Salad, page 78
Bagwell's Opakapaka, page 115
Garnish with Kiwi and Orange slices
Strawberries Romanoff, page 172

Chicken Party Rolls

2-3 cups seasoned bread stuffing, crushed with	2 cups cooked chicken
1/2 t. poultry seasoning	1 (4 oz.) can chopped mushrooms, drained
1 (8 oz.) pkg. cream cheese	2 cylinders (8 servings each) crescent rolls
4 T. soft butter	
1/2 t. pepper	

Combine cream cheese, butter, and pepper until smooth. Stir in chicken and mushrooms. Separate 16 rolls and divide chicken filling into 16 balls. Roll up ends tucking in the sides. You will need to stretch the dough. Roll in melted butter, then in bread crumbs. Place on ungreased baking sheets, leaving an inch between each ball. Bake at 350° for about 20 minutes on highest oven rack. Serve with chicken giblet gravy. Yield: 8 servings.

Chicken Scallopini

4 chicken breasts, skinned and boned	1 T. butter
	1 T. salad oil

Sauce:

1/3 cup dry white wine or chicken broth	1 t. lemon juice
1/4 cup whipping cream	1/4 t. thyme leaves

Place meat between sheets of waxed paper and with a wooden mallet pound evenly and gently until about 1/4 inch thick. Dust meat with flour and shake off excess. In a wide pan over medium-high heat, melt 1 T. butter and salad oil.

Quickly cook the chicken about 1 1/2 minutes per side or just until meat loses its pinkness when slashed. Place on a platter and keep warm. Add 1/3 cup wine or chicken broth, stirring to blend in browned particles. Boil until reduced by about half. Add whipping cream, lemon juice, and thyme leaves; boil until sauce thickens slightly. Pour any meat juices that collected on serving platter into sauce. Salt and pepper to taste. Pour over meat and garnish with parsley and lemon wedges. Yield: 4 servings.

Chicken with Basil

3 - 4   **T. seeded and finely chopped, canned green chiles**
  2   **T. soy sauce**
  1   **t. sugar**
  1   **t. vinegar**
  $^1/_2$ **cup chopped fresh basil or 2 T. dried basil**
  1   **t. chopped fresh mint or $^1/_4$ t. dry mint**
  $^1/_2$ **t. cornstarch**
  1   **clove garlic, minced or pressed**
  2   **lb. chicken breasts, skinned, boned, cut in $^1/_4$ x 2 inch strips**
  1   **large onion, cut in $^1/_4$ inch slices**

Mix together chiles, soy, sugar, vinegar, basil, mint, and cornstarch; set aside.

Place wok on high heat. When wok is hot, add $1^1/_2$ T. of oil. When oil is hot, add garlic and half the chicken; stir-fry until chicken is opaque (about 3 minutes); remove from wok and set aside. Repeat with remaining chicken, adding oil as needed. Reheat wok and add 1 T. oil. Add onion and stir-fry until limp about 1 minute. Add chile mixture and return chicken to wok; stir until sauce boils and thickens slightly (about 1 minute). Yield: 3-4 servings.

Chicken with 40 Garlic Cloves

  $^2/_3$ **cup olive oil**
  8   **chicken legs, remove skin**
  8   **chicken thighs, remove skin**
  4   **ribs celery, chopped**
  2   **medium onions, chopped**

  4   **T. flat-leaf parsley, chopped**
  1   **T. fresh tarragon**
40   **cloves garlic, unpeeled**
  2   **loaves French bread**

Put olive oil in shallow dish and coat chicken pieces with it. Cover bottom of heavy 6 quart casserole with mixture of celery and onion. Add parsley and tarragon. Lay chicken pieces on top. Salt and pepper. Intersperse garlic cloves with chicken pieces. Cover tightly with foil and lid. Bake at 375° for $1^1/_2$ hours without peeking.

Can also be made in a crockpot on low for 8 hours. Yield: 16 servings.

Serve chicken pieces, pan juices, and garlic cloves with thin slices of hot French bread. Garlic may be squeezed from its husk and spread on bread like butter.

Lemon Chicken

3 lbs. boneless chicken breasts	$^1/_3$ cup sugar
1 T. sherry	1 T. cornstarch
1 T. soy sauce	1 cup chicken broth
$^1/_2$ t. salt	1 T. lemon juice
2 eggs	1 t. salt
$^1/_4$ cup cornstarch	2 T. vegetable oil
$^1/_2$ t. baking powder	1 lemon, thinly sliced
2 cups vegetable oil	

Combine chicken with sherry, soy sauce and salt. Marinate for 15 minutes. Beat eggs, cornstarch, and baking powder to form a smooth batter. Heat oil to 350°. Coat chicken with batter and fry until brown. Cut into 1 by 1$^1/_2$ inch pieces and arrange on a serving dish. Combine sugar, 1 T. cornstarch, broth, lemon juice, and salt. Heat remaining oil. Stir-fry the lemon slices for 30 seconds. Slowly stir in cornstarch mixture. Cook, stirring constantly, until sauce is clear. Pour over chicken and serve immediately. Yield: 6-8 servings.

Mexican Chicken Breasts

6 chicken breasts, deboned, skinless
  chunky picante sauce
4 T. lime juice

Marinate breasts in picante sauce and lime juice. Brown breasts in a skillet; add marinade and cook covered for 30 minutes on simmer.

Serve on a plate with sour cream and chopped fresh cilantro sprinkled on top. Yield: 6 servings.

Oven Fried Chicken with Herbs

6-8	pieces frying chicken	¹/₂	t. pepper
¹/₂	cup flour	¹/₂	t. thyme
2	t. salt	2	T. grated onion
³/₄	cup Crisco	¹/₂	t. salt
1	clove garlic, minced		

Flour and salt chicken. Brown in ¹/₂ cup Crisco. Then arrange them one layer deep in a shallow baking pan. In a small saucepan, combine ¹/₄ cup Crisco and other remaining ingredients. Bring to a boil and pour over chicken in baking pan. Cover and bake at 350° for one hour until tender.

Tastes and smells like a stuffed baking chicken. Salt goes all the way through and is very tender. Yield: 6-8 servings.

Quesadillas

¹/₂	lb. Monterey Jack cheese, grated
¹/₂	lb. Cheddar cheese, grated
1	small can hot Jalapeño peppers
1	(28 oz.) can stewed tomatoes
1	small onion, diced
1	pkg. flour tortillas
	sour cream
	salt and pepper

Mix stewed tomatoes, onion, Jalapeño peppers, salt and pepper together and refrigerate over night.

Place about ¹/₄ cup of combined grated cheeses on ¹/₂ of each tortilla. Fold each tortilla in half and fry in ¹/₄" deep bacon grease or oil.

Serve with hot tomato mixture and sour cream on top. Yield: 6-8 servings.

Shake and Bake

4	cups bread crumbs	1	T. paprika
¹/₂	cup oil	1	t. pepper
1	T. salt		

Combine ingredients and store in airtight container in refrigerator. Use mixture on chicken, pork chops, and fish. Yield: 4 cups.

Slivered Chicken and Walnuts

1	lb. chicken breast, skinned boned, cut into small pieces	¹/₂	cup walnut halves
1	T. soy sauce	1	medium size green pepper, seeded and cut into 1 in. squares
1	t. cornstarch	¹/₂	t. fresh ginger root, minced
3	T. salad oil		

Prepare the following cooking sauce and set aside:

1 t. cornstarch

dash liquid hot pepper seasoning

1¹/₂ t. each sugar and wine vinegar

2 t. dry sherry or water

2 T. soy sauce

Mix chicken pieces with soy and cornstarch and set aside.

Place wok over medium-high heat. When wok is hot, add oil. When oil is hot, add walnuts and stir-fry until brown (about 1 minute); remove walnuts with a slotted spoon and set aside. Add chicken to oil and stir-fry until chicken is opaque (about 3 minutes); remove from wok and set aside.

Add green pepper and ginger and stir-fry until pepper is tender-crisp (about 1 minute). Add chicken and cooking sauce, stirring until it boils and thickens (about 1 minute). Stir in walnuts. Yield: 2 servings.

Beef and Pork

Beef Scallopini with Capers

Beef Tenderloin

Beef Stroganoff

Chili

East Indian Sate

Easy Leg of Lamb

Flank Marinade

Flank Steak, Slices

Ginger Beef

Hamburger Cashew Casserole

Hamburger Casserole

Indonesian Sate

Italian Stew

Marinade for Korean Shortribs

Oyster Beef

Pork, Garlic, and Vegetable Stir-Fry

Pork Scallopini with Mustard Cream

Steak Lorraine

Super Nachos

Teriyaki Marinade for Beef

Beef Scallopini with Capers

³/₄ lb. boneless sirloin, rib, or sirloin tip	1 T. butter
	1 T. oil

Sauce:

3 T. shallot or green onion, finely chopped	¹/₄ t. dry mustard
1 cup thinly sliced mushrooms	1¹/₂ t. capers, drained
¹/₂ cup beef broth	¹/₂ t. each Worcestershire sauce and lemon juice
3 T. brandy (optional)	

Place meat between sheets of plastic wrap or waxed paper and, with a heavy wooden mallet, pound meat evenly until about ¹/₄ inch thick. Cook immediately or place slices side by side on waxed paper; roll, then wrap well and chill up to 1 day.

Dust meat with flour and shake off excess. In a wide frying pan over medium-high heat, place butter and oil. When butter melts, add as many meat pieces as will fit without crowding and cook quickly about 1 minute per side, just until browned and pink inside when slashed. Place on a hot platter and keep warm. Cook remaining pieces, adding more butter and oil as needed. Place on platter and keep warm.

Add onion and mushrooms, sauté until limp. Add broth, mustard, capers, Worcestershire sauce, and lemon juice. Boil until reduced to about half. Pour any meat juices that collected on serving platter into sauce, add salt and pepper to taste, and pour over meat. Garnish with chopped parsley or thinly sliced green onion. Yield: 4 servings.

Beef Tenderloin

2 lb. beef tenderloin

Rub with oil, salt, and pepper and place on a racked pan. Preheat oven to 425° and cook in center of oven for 30-45 minutes. For medium rare, cook for 40 minutes. Remove from oven and let stand 10 minutes before slicing into ¹/₄ - ¹/₂ inch slices. Serve with Bearnaise Sauce (pg. 83). Yield: 6-8 servings.

Beef Stroganoff

1	T. flour	1	clove garlic, minced
½	t. salt	2	T. butter
1	lb. beef sirloin, cut	3	T. flour
	in ¼ inch wide strips	1	T. tomato paste
2	T. butter	1¼	cups beef stock
1	cup sliced mushrooms	1	cup sour cream
½	cup chopped onion	2	T. cream sherry

Dredge meat strips in flour and salt combination. Melt 2 T. butter in a skillet and add meat, browning quickly. Add mushrooms, onion, garlic; cook 3-4 minutes.

Remove meat and vegetables from skillet. Add 2 T. butter to pan drippings; when melted, blend in 3 T. flour. Add tomato paste.

Slowly pour in cold meat stock and cook, stirring constantly, until mixture thickens. Return meat and vegetables to skillet. Stir in sour cream and sherry; heat briefly. Serve with rice or noodles. Yield: 4-5 servings.

Chili

2	lb. ground beef	2	cans kidney beans, (1 lb. each)
2	cups chopped onions		drain and reserve liquid
2	cans tomatoes	¼	cup Jalapeño peppers, chopped
	(1 lb. 12 oz. each)	1½ - 2	T. chili powder
1	can tomato sauce (8 oz.)	2	t. salt
1	T. sugar		

Brown meat and onions in large kettle. Drain fat. Stir in tomatoes, tomato sauce, liquid from kidney beans, Jalapeño peppers, and seasonings. Simmer uncovered 45 minutes stirring occasionally. Stir in beans and simmer 15 minutes. Yield: 6-8 servings.

East Indian Sate

1	T. ground coriander
1	T. salt
$^1/_2$	t. freshly ground pepper
1	cup chopped onion
2	cloves garlic, peeled
$^1/_2$	cup soy sauce
$^1/_4$	cup lime or lemon juice
$^1/_2$	cup peanut butter
$^1/_4$	cup brown sugar
$^1/_2$	cup peanut or salad oil
	Dash cayenne or liquid hot-pepper seasoning
2	lb. meat (boneless veal leg or shoulder, or boned chicken) cut into one inch cubes

Combine coriander, salt, pepper, onion, garlic, soy sauce, lemon juice, peanut butter, brown sugar, oil, and seasoning. Whirl smooth in a blender. Marinate the meat in this mixture for 1-2 hours. String on skewers. Grill over hot coals until brown but not dry, about 3-4 minutes on each side. Serve with the remaining marinade. Yield: 6-8 servings.

Easy Leg of Lamb

1	short-cut leg of lamb (5-6 lb.)	1	t. salt
4	cloves garlic, split	4	T. melted butter
$^1/_2$	t. crumbled dried oregano		juice of 1 lemon

Make several cuts in the leg of lamb and insert garlic and a mixture of the oregano and salt. With any remaining oregano and salt, rub the outside of the meat. Insert the slit almost parallel to the bone and place on rotisserie over medium coals. Mix melted butter and lemon juice and brush on meat. Basting once or twice, barbecue 1$^1/_4$ to 1$^1/_2$ hours (140°-150° on meat thermometer) for medium rare. Yield: 6-8 servings.

Flank Marinade

1¹/₂ lb. flank steak
1 cup apple juice
1 cup soy sauce

Mix together. Marinate steak for 2 hours. Broil or grill steak 5 minutes per side. Slice on the diagonal. Yield: 4-6 servings.

Flank Steak, Slices

1 flank steak, 1¹/₂-2 lbs.   1 clove garlic, crushed
¹/₄ cup salad oil   ¹/₂ t. salt
1 T. lemon juice   ¹/₄ t. pepper

Combine salad oil, lemon juice, garlic, salt and pepper for marinade. Place steak in plastic bag or flat dish and pour marinade over it. Close bag securely or cover dish with foil and refrigerate 4-6 hours or overnight, turning occasionally. Pour off and reserve marinade.

Place steak on grill three to four inches from coals and broil for 5 minutes. Turn, brush with marinade, and broil 5 minutes longer or to desired doneness. Carve by slicing diagonally across grain into thin strips. Yield: 4 servings.

"Slightly freeze uncooked meat for easier slicing when you are stir-frying, making teriyaki, or kabobs."

"Turn meat with tongs, instead of a fork, to avoid losing meat juices."

Pork, Garlic, and Vegetable Stir-Fry

$1^1/_4$ **lb. pork tenderloin**

3   **T. jalapeño pepper, minced**

3   **T. soy sauce**

$1^1/_2$ **t. grated lime rind**

3   **T. fresh lime juice**

$^1/_4$ **t. salt**

9   **cloves garlic, minced**

$^3/_4$ **lb. fresh green beans**

1   **cup julienne-cut (2 inch) carrots**

2   **t. oil, divided**

1   **t. cornstarch**

$^1/_2$ **cup chicken broth**

8   **cups hot, cooked rice.**

Trim fat from pork and cut pork in half lengthwise. Cut each half crosswise into $^1/_4$ inch thick slices; set aside.

To make sauce: combine pepper and next 5 ingredients in a bowl. Pour $^1/_4$ cup sauce mixture into a large zip-top plastic bag. Add pork; seal bag and marinate in refrigerator 30 minutes, turning occasionally.

Wash beans; trim ends and remove strings. Cut into 2 inch pieces. Place remaining sauce mixture in a large zip-top plastic bag. Add beans and carrots; seal bag and marinate in refrigerator 30 minutes; turning occasionally.

In a wok add 1 t. oil. Place over medium-high heat. Add pork mixture; stir-fry 3 minutes. Remove pork from skillet; set aside. Add remaining teaspoon oil to wok; place over medium-hight heat. Add bean mixture; stir-fry 10 minutes or until crisp-tender.

Place cornstarch in a bowl; gradually add broth, stirring until blended. Return pork to wok and add the broth mixture and stir-fry 3 minutes or until pork is tender and liquid is thickened. Add vegetables and serve over rice. Yield: 6 servings.

Pork Scallopini with Mustard Cream

$^1/_2$-$^3/_4$ lb. thin boneless pork chops
1 T. butter
1 T. oil

Sauce:
$^1/_3$ cup dry vermouth or chicken broth
$^1/_2$ t. lemon juice
$^1/_4$ cup whipping cream
1 T. Dijon mustard
dash of nutmeg

Place meat between sheets of waxed paper and with a wooden mallet, pound evenly and gently until about $^1/_4$ inch thick. Dust meat with flour and shake off excess. In a wide pan over medium high heat, melt butter and oil. Quickly cook the pork about $1^1/_2$ minutes per side or just until pork is lightly browned and no longer pink when slashed. Place on a platter and keep warm.

Pour $^1/_3$ cup dry vermouth or chicken broth and lemon juice into pan; stir to blend in browned particles. Boil until reduced to about half. Stir in whipping cream, mustard and nutmeg. Bring sauce to a boil and cook, stirring, until sauce thickens slightly.

Pour any meat juices that collected on serving platter into sauce, add salt and pepper to taste, and pour over meat. Garnish with chopped parsley. Yield: 2 servings.

"For a fluffier meat loaf, add about $^1/_2$ teaspoon
of baking powder to every pound
of meat mixture before baking."

Steak Lorraine

1	clove garlic, peeled and sliced	$^1/_2$	t. salt
$^1/_4$	cup salad oil	$^1/_4$	cup chopped parsley
4	(8 oz.) boneless sirloin steaks	2	t. lemon juice
$^1/_4$	cup butter or margarine	1	t. Worcestershire sauce
1	t. dry mustard	$^1/_4$	t. ground pepper

Combine garlic and oil; let stand for 5 minutes. Brush steak on both sides with garlic/oil mixture. Stir butter, mustard and salt together in heavy skillet. Stir in parsley; heat until butter bubbles. Place steak in skillet. Turn over to coat both sides. Cook slowly for 5 minutes; do not brown. Turn steaks; cook for 5 more minutes. Remove steaks to hot platter. Add lemon juice, Worcestershire sauce, and pepper. Heat and stir to blend. Pour over steaks. Serve at once. Yield: 4 servings.

Super Nachos

Sauté 1 lb. lean **ground beef** and 1 large **chopped onion** until lightly browned. Discard fat, season with **salt**. Add **liquid hot pepper** seasoning to taste. Spread 1 or 2 cans (11 oz. each) **refried beans** in shallow 10 x 15 pan or oven proof dish. Top evenly with meat mixture. Chop 1 (4 oz.) can of **whole chiles**. Sprinkle chiles over bean and meat mixture. Cover evenly with 2-3 cups **shredded Jack or Cheddar cheese** or combination. Measure $^3/_4$ cup prepared **taco sauce** (red or green) and drizzle over cheese. Can be made ahead, then cover and refrigerate.

Bake uncovered in 400° oven for 20-25 minutes or until very hot. Sprinkle with $^1/_4$ cup chopped **green onion**, 1 cup pitted **ripe olives**. In center top put 1 can thawed **avocado dip** or 1 medium coarsely mashed avocado. Top with about 1 cup **sour cream.** Yield: 4-6 servings.

Serve with 8 cups **tortilla chips**; SCOOP and enjoy.

Teriyaki Marinade for Beef

$^3/_4$ **cup soy sauce**

$^1/_4$ **sugar**

2 **T. each of Whiskey and sesame oil**

1 **large garlic clove, crushed**

1 **T. chopped fresh ginger or 1 t. ground ginger**

Yield: $^3/_4$ cup, enough marinade for $1^1/_2$ - 2 pounds of beef.

Winter Dinner For Eight

Hot Cider Punch, page 19
Cheese-Filled Phyllo Triangles, page 23
Cream of Broccoli Soup, page 38
Lavosh, page 59
Bibb Lettuce with
Tarragon Mustard Vinaigrette, page 92
Beef Tenderloin, page 141
Bearnaise Sauce, page 85
Twice-Baked Potatoes, page 111
Carrots and Tarragon, page 97
Fudge Nut Pie, page 190

Light Winter Dinner

Minestrone Soup, page 42
Beer Bread, page 51
Make Ahead Caesar Salad, page 73
Carrot Cake, page 177

Pasta

Carbonara

Fresh Tomato Pasta

Lasagna Minus Pasta

Lasagna Roll-ups

Linguine with Scallops in Cream Sauce

Pesto

Simple Alfredo

Spaghetti Pie

Carbonara

¹/₄	lb. mild Italian pork sausage
¹/₂	lb. prosciutto or cooked ham (thinly sliced)
2	T. butter or margarine
¹/₂	cup lightly packed minced parsley
3	eggs, beaten
¹/₂	cup freshly grated Parmesan cheese
1	8 oz. pkg. spaghetti, cooked

Remove casings from sausage; crumble sausage.

Place wok over medium heat. When wok is hot, add sausage and half the prosciutto or ham; stir-fry for about 5 minutes or until lightly browned. Blend remaining half of proscuitto with cooked sausage mixture; remove wok from heat. Drain fat.

Add hot spaghetti, butter, and parsley to meats. Mix quickly to blend. At once pour in eggs and continue to blend, quickly lifting and mixing the pasta to coat well with egg. Sprinkle in the ¹/₂ cup cheese and a dash of pepper; mix again. Serve with additional cheese. Yield: 4 servings.

"Put a tablespoon of oil in the water to keep spaghetti and macaroni from boiling over and from sticking together."

"Small amounts of tomato paste can be frozen on a sheet of foil. Remove from foil and store in plastic bags until needed."

"Use a large green pepper as a container for dip. Just cut off the top and remove the seeds."

Fresh Tomato Pasta

Make early in the day and let it SIT.

Cook 6 cloves thinly sliced garlic in olive oil (on LOW for 10 plus minutes)
Pour in a large ceramic bowl.

Add: **lots of fresh, chopped tomatoes or a large can Italian plum tomatoes**
   3 **T. red wine vinegar**
     lots of freshly chopped parsley
     some basil
     lots of red pepper flakes

Cook **1 box capellini**, drain and fold into sauce. Heat to serving temperature.
Serve with salad and hot bread. Grate fresh Parmesan cheese and pass it at the table. Yield 6-8 servings.
All you cook is the garlic and pasta!

Lasagna Minus Pasta

1¹/₂	**lb. ground beef**	¹/₈	**t. garlic salt**
2	**T. oil**	1	**small can tomato paste**
³/₄	**cup chopped onion**	1	**cup cottage cheese**
1	**T. parsley flakes**	1	**egg, beaten**
¹/₂	**t. oregano**	¹/₃	**cup Parmesan cheese**
¹/₂	**t. salt**	2	**slices mozzarella cheese**
¹/₄	**t. pepper**	1	**can crescent dinner rolls**
¹/₄	**t. thyme**		**milk & sesame seeds**

Brown meat. Drain off fat. Add next nine ingredients. Mix cottage cheese with egg and Parmesan cheese. Place meat in a 9 x 13 inch casserole. Put cottage cheese mixture on top. Place mozzarella cheese slices on top. Cover all with crescent roll dough, like a crust. Brush dough with milk and sprinkle with sesame seeds.
Bake at 325° for 20 minutes. Yield: 6-8 servings.

Lasagna Roll-ups

8	lasagna noodles (cooked)	1	(10 oz.) pkg. frozen spinach
1	T. olive oil		(thawed and well drained)
2	large garlic cloves	1¹/₂	cups mozzarella cheese, grated
1	cup ricotta cheese	1	(14 oz.) jar spaghetti sauce
1	t. salt		

Cook lasagna noodles and lay flat. Heat oil and sauté garlic for 2 minutes or until tender, on low. Combine ricotta cheese, spinach, salt, garlic, and half of the mozzarella cheese.

Spread ¹/₄ cup of spinach mixture on each of the noodles. Roll noodle up firmly. Pour spaghetti sauce into pan and place roll-ups, seam side down in the sauce. Bring to a boil, then reduce heat and simmer for 5 minutes. Sprinkle roll-ups with rest of mozzarella. Cover and simmer 3-5 minutes. Yield: 8 servings.

Can be made a day before or freeze. Great for a quick meal or snack.

Linguine with Scallops in Cream Sauce

¹/₄	lb. sea scallops	1	small onion,
3	T. margarine		finely chopped
10	oz. mushrooms	¹/₄	t. salt

In a wok saute 2 T. margarine with salt, onion, and mushrooms and then remove from pan.

In wok melt 1 T. margarine and cook sea scallops 2-3 minutes. Return mushroom mixture to wok.

Stir in:

¹/₄	cup half and half	¹/₂	t. pepper
1	T. sherry (dry)	³/₄	t. salt

Heat to boiling over high heat.

Stir in: ¹/₂ **lb. fresh spinach, thinly sliced and 1 pint cherry tomatoes**, cut in half. Cook **1 lb. pkg. linguine**. Toss with scallop mixture. Yield: 6 servings.

Pesto

4-6	garlic cloves, chopped
2	cups fresh basil leaves
6	T. grated Parmesan cheese
$^1/_4$	cup chopped pine nuts or walnuts
$^1/_2$	t. salt
$^1/_2$	cup olive oil (do not substitute)

In electric blender or food processor, blend all ingredients except the oil to a smooth paste. Slowly blend in oil and stir until smooth. Serve with hot pasta.

Place leftovers in a small jar, covered with 1 tablespoon olive oil, and refrigerate. Yield: 1 cup.

Simple Alfredo

1	cup half and half
1	cup whipping cream
3	T. freshly grated Parmesan cheese
2	T. freshly grated Romano cheese
	salt and white pepper
1	lb. shrimp, shelled and deveined
1	lb. scallops
1	lb. pasta bows (cooked)

Heat the first five ingredients in a wok. Add the shrimp and scallops. Cook on medium for a few minutes. Add 1 lb. cooked pasta bows which have been rinsed in cold water after cooking al dente. Yield: 6-8 servings.

157

Spaghetti Pie

¹/₂ (12 oz.) pkg. vermicelli
2 T. butter or margarine
¹/₃ cup grated Parmesan cheese
2 eggs, well beaten
1 lb. ground beef
¹/₂ cup chopped onion
¹/₄ cup chopped green pepper
1 (8 oz.) can stewed tomatoes, undrained
1 (6 oz.) can tomato paste
1 t. sugar
³/₄ t. dried whole oregano
¹/₂ t. salt
¹/₂ t. garlic salt
1 cup cream-style cottage cheese
¹/₂ cup shredded mozzarella cheese
8-10 pepperoni slices

Cook vermicelli according to package directions; drain. Stir butter and Parmesan cheese into hot vermicelli. Add eggs, stirring well. Spoon mixture into a 10 inch pie plate. Use a spoon to shape the spaghetti into a pie shell. Microwave on HIGH, uncovered, 3 minutes or until set. Set aside.

Crumble beef in a shallow 2 quart casserole; stir in onion and green pepper. Cover with plastic wrap, and microwave on HIGH 5-6 minutes, stirring at 2 minute intervals; drain well. Stir in tomatoes, tomato paste, and seasonings. Cover and microwave on HIGH 3-4 minutes, stirring once, set aside.

Spread cottage cheese evenly over pie shell. Top with meat sauce. Cover with plastic wrap, and microwave on HIGH for 6 minutes; sprinkle with mozzarella cheese. Microwave, uncovered on HIGH for 30 seconds or until cheese begins to melt. Garnish with pepperoni. Microwave, uncovered on HIGH 1 minute. Let stand 10 minutes before serving. Yield: 8 servings.

Desserts *to die for....*

The Dead House, a 1700's mausoleum, is located down the path from Quarters A.

Desserts to die for...

Amaretto Freeze

Amaretto Sauce

Burnt Creme

Cantaloupe Delight

Cantaloupe Whip

Chess Tarts

Chocolate Pots de Creme

Coeur a la Creme with Berries

Fancy Flan

Fresh Strawberry Sorbet

Haupia • Ice Cream

Marble-ous Frozen Peanut Butter Dessert

Microwave Creme Brulee

Nut Mosaic Tart

Pavlova

Pots de Creme

Raspberry Fluff

Raspberry Yum-Yum from "The Lake"

Rhubarb Delight

Rice Pudding • Shortbread

Strawberries Romanoff

Vanilla Pudding

Amaretto Freeze

¹/₃ **cup amaretto**
1 **T. brown sugar**
1 **quart vanilla ice cream**

Combine amaretto and brown sugar; stir until sugar dissolves.

Combine ice cream and amaretto mixture in food processor or blender; process until smooth. Pour into 6 individual freezer proof serving dishes and freeze.

Garnish with whipped cream and maraschino cherries just before serving, if desired. Yield: 6 servings.

"If you need superfine sugar, process granulated sugar in a blender or food processor."

"Nuts freeze well in plastic bags."

Amaretto Sauce

²/₃ **cup light brown sugar**   ¹/₄ **cup half-half**
¹/₄ **cup butter**   2 **T. light corn syrup**

Cook in the microwave oven on HIGH for 2 minutes. Stir. Cook on high for another 1-3 minutes until mixture comes to a boil.

Stir in:

2 **T. Amaretto**   1 **cup chopped almonds**

Cook on high for one minute. Yield: 2 cups.

Burnt Creme

1   **pint whipping cream**
4   **egg yolks**
¹/₂ **cup granulated sugar**
1   **T. vanilla**

Preheat oven to 350 degrees. Heat cream over low heat until bubbles form around edge of pan. Beat egg yolks and sugar together until thick and yellow (about 2-3 minutes). While beating constantly, pour cream in steady stream into the egg yolks. Add vanilla and pour into custard cups. Place custard cups in baking pan that has about an inch of boiling water in the bottom. Bake for 45 minutes. Remove custard cups from water and refrigerate until chilled. Sprinkle each custard cup with granulated sugar. Place on top rack under broiler and cook until sugar topping is medium brown. Refrigerate before serving. Yield: 6 servings.

Cantaloupe Delight

1   **T. finely chopped**   4   **cups cantaloupe balls**
    crystallized ginger   1   **cup ginger ale, chilled**
1   **t. grated lime rind**   **Garnish: fresh mint leaves**
2   **T. lime juice**

Combine ginger, lime rind, and lime juice; pour over cantaloupe balls. Cover and chill 8 hours. To serve, spoon into stemmed glasses, and pour ginger ale evenly over each serving. Garnish with mint leaves, if desired. Yield: 4-6 servings.

Cantaloupe Whip

2 1/4   **cups cubed cantaloupe**
1   **T. lemon juice**
2   **egg whites**
1/4   **cup sugar**

Place a single layer of cantaloupe in a shallow pan; freeze until firm. Drop cantaloupe through food chute of food processor or blender with motor running. Add lemon juice and process until mixture is smooth.

Beat egg whites (at room temperature) in a small bowl at high speed with electric mixer until foamy; gradually add sugar, 1 tablespoon at a time, beating until stiff peaks form. Fold into cantaloupe mixture. Spoon into an 8 inch square pan and freeze until firm. Let stand at room temperature 10 minutes before serving. Yield: 4 servings.

Chess Tarts

2   **cups sugar**
1   **stick butter**
4   **eggs**
1   **t. vinegar**

1   **T. flour**
1 1/2   **T. milk**
1/4   **t. salt**
  juice of one lemon

Cream butter and sugar. Add rest of ingredients, mixing well. Place small amounts in uncooked **tart shells**. (Bama shells in the frozen food section). Cook in a 350° oven for 20 minutes or until brown. Serve with whipped cream on top. Yield: 12 servings.

Chocolate Pots de Creme

2	cups milk	2	t. vanilla
2	eggs		dash of salt
2	T. sugar	2	cups semi-sweet chocolate bits
4	t. cognac, rum		
	or Grand Marnier		

Heat the milk just to the boiling point. Place all other ingredients in order listed in blender. Add the hot milk and blend at low speed for 1 minute. Pour into 4 oz. or 6 oz. serving containers—souffle molds, custard cups, or pots de creme pots and refrigerate for a few hours. Yield: 4-6 servings.

Coeur a la Creme With Berries

(Prepare at least a day ahead; serve within 1 to 2 days)

4	cups (2 pints) sour cream	1	cup sugar
6	egg yolks	3-4	strips lemon peel
1	(8 oz.) pkg. cream cheese		Strawberries

In the top of a boiler heat sour cream, stirring, until scalding (180 degrees). Blend some of the hot cream with the egg yolks thoroughly beaten with cream cheese and sugar. Return all to double broiler. Add lemon peel. Cook over simmering water, stirring frequently, until thickened, about 15 minutes.

Remove from heat. Cover and let stand in the hot water for 15 minutes more; discard lemon peel. Line a large wire strainer or colander (or coeur a la creme mold) with 3 or 4 thicknesses of cheesecloth; arrange over another pan for draining. Pour in cheese mixture. Let stand about 2 hours at room temperature; then gently draw up loose edges of cheesecloth and fasten lightly over cheese. Continue draining while it chills overnight. (If you do not use the heart-shaped mold, cheese can be shaped with a spatula.) To serve: unmold and garnish with strawberries. Yield: 3 cups.

Fancy Flan

Prepare 1 box of **Jello Flan** according to directions. Invert on a plate. Top with **whipped cream** and fresh **raspberries** on the side for garnish. Yield: 6-8 servings.

Fresh Strawberry Sorbet

²/₃ cup sugar
²/₃ cup water
2¹/₂ pints ripe strawberries, puréed and chilled
2 T. fresh lemon juice

Combine sugar and water in small saucepan over medium-high heat and stir until sugar is dissolved. Just before syrup comes to boil, remove from heat. Cool and chill. Add syrup to remaining ingredients and blend well. Finish in ice cream maker or freezer. If frozen in a freezer without a special machine, they must be placed in a metal container (in an 8 inch layer cake pan is ideal for 1 quart) for fast freezing. After they are frozen, they must be partially thawed, then beaten in a food processor using the steel knife. They should be made as needed, preferably within 24 hours. Store in airtight plastic containers. One hour before serving, remove from freezer and place in refrigerator for optimum flavor and texture. Makes 1 quart. Yield: 15 servings.

Haupia

12 oz. frozen coconut milk   ¹/₂ cup plus 2 T. sugar
1¹/₂ cups water   ¹/₂ cup plus 2 T. cornstarch

Combine all ingredients in saucepan. Stir over medium heat until thickened. Lower heat and cook for 10 minutes, stirring constantly to avoid lumping or burning. Pour into 8 x 8 inch dish and chill until set. Cut haupia into squares. Note: May be topped with crushed pineapple, sliced peaches, or sliced mango. Yield: 6-8 servings.

Ice Cream

2	cups whole milk	2	eggs, beaten
6	T. sugar	1	t. vanilla
¹/₄	cup light corn syrup		

Blend and pour in ice cube tray. When frozen about one hour, remove from freezer and beat again. Return to freezer and leave until frozen hard. May add 1 banana or 1 cup of strawberries, if desired. Yield: 4 servings.

"To avoid 'lumps': pour wet ingredients into dry ingredients."
"Mix together: 1 cup minus 1 T. milk and 1 T. white vinegar to substitute for 1 cup buttermilk."

Marble-ous Frozen Peanut Butter Dessert

¹/₂	cup packed brown sugar	¹/₄	cup margarine
¹/₂	cup peanut butter	1	cup flour

Cream together and put ¹/₂ into a 9 x 13 inch dish and bake for 10-15 minutes in a 350° oven or microwave 3 minutes on HIGH.

1	(8 oz.) pkg. cream cheese	1	t. vanilla
¹/₂	cup sugar	2	eggs
¹/₄	cup peanut butter	1	cup whipped cream

Combine and pour over cooled crumb crust.

1 (6 oz.) pkg. chocolate chips

Melt chips and drizzle over filling and marble. Sprinkle reserved crumbs on top. Freeze at least two hours. Yield: 12 servings.

Microwave Creme Brulee

1¹/₂ **cups milk**	¹/₂ **cup sugar**
3 **eggs yolks**	6 **T. light brown sugar,**
1 **T. vanilla**	**for caramelized tops**

Heat milk in a 4 cup glass measure, uncovered, on HIGH for 4 minutes.

Remove from oven. Whisk together egg yolks, sugar, and vanilla until well combined. Whisking constantly, add hot milk in a thin stream. Divide mixture evenly among six ¹/₂ cup ramekins.

Place ramekins in a shallow ceramic dish just large enough to hold them without touching. Pour water around them to a depth of 1 inch. Cook, uncovered on HIGH for 6-8 minutes. Do not overcook because the custards will still be wet at center.

Remove from oven and set ramekins on a cooling rack. When completely cool, refrigerate for at least 6 hours.

Preheat broiler. Sift 1¹/₂ T. brown sugar over each custard, completely covering the top. Fit ramekins into a metal pan. Fill gaps between ramekins with ice and add water to a depth of ¹/₂ inch.

Broil just until sugar melts, about 4 minutes. Watch carefully to avoid burning. Remove from oven and rub each caramel crust with ice for 30 seconds, to harden it. Do not refrigerate once the tops have been broiled, as caramel crust will soften and liquefy. Yield: 6 servings.

 Italian Delight

Green Salad with Classic Vinaigrette, page 92
Spaghetti with Pesto, page 157
Fried Eggplant, page 99
French Bread, page 56
Ice Cream, page 166 with Amaretto Sauce, page 161

Nut Mosaic Tart

Serve warm, or make ahead and let stand overnight—or freeze for up to a month.

3 **cups whole or half nuts** (almonds, walnuts, filberts, macadamias, pistachios, or pecans — if salted, place nuts in a towel and rub off salt.)

3 **eggs**

1 **cup honey**

$^1/_2$ **t. grated orange peel**

1 **t. vanilla**

$^1/_4$ **cup butter or margarine, melted**

sweetened whipped cream (optional)

butter pastry (recipe follows)

Place nuts (if unroasted) in a shallow pan and put in a 350° oven until lightly toasted, about 10 minutes; let cool. Press butter pastry evenly over bottom and sides of 11 inch tart pan with removable bottom.

In a bowl, combine eggs, honey, orange peel, vanilla, and melted butter; beat well until blended. Stir in roasted nuts. Pour into pastry-lined tart pan. Bake on bottom rack of a 350° oven until top is golden brown all over, about 40 minutes. Let cool on a wire rack. Remove pan sides. Offer wedges with whipped cream. Yield: 10-12 servings.

Butter Pastry

Combine **1$^1/_3$ cups all purpose flour, 3 tablespoons sugar, and $^1/_2$ cup butter or margarine,** cut into pieces. Whirl in a food processor or rub between your fingers until coarse crumbs form. Add **1 egg yolk**; process or stir until dough sticks together.

Pavlova

4   egg whites
1¹/₂   cups sugar
1   t. cornstarch
1   t. lemon juice or white wine vinegar
1   t. vanilla
    sweetened whipped cream
    strawberries, bananas, or fruit salad

Beat egg whites as stiffly as possible, until peaks form and stand up. Gradually add sugar and beat after each addition. Add sifted cornstarch, lemon juice, and vanilla. Mixture must be very stiff. Mark a circle of the size required on a sheet of foil or paper placed on a board or baking sheet. With the meringue, shape a shell with 2 or 3 inch sides and a saucer-shaped center. Bake at 300° for 1 hour. Turn oven off and leave in the cooling oven for another hour. Meringue should be firm and may be slightly colored. Place on a serving dish. Fill center with whipped cream and cover cream with strawberries, bananas, or fruit salad. Yield: 6-8 servings.

Pots de Creme

1   (6 oz.) pkg. semi-sweet chocolate pieces
¹/₂   cup brewed coffee
4   eggs
3   T. sugar
³/₄-1   t. brandy or rum extract

Blend chocolate pieces at medium blender speed. Add coffee; blend 5 seconds, add eggs, sugar, extract and blend until smooth, about 40 seconds. Pour into 6 pot de creme cups. Refrigerate overnight. Garnish with whipped cream. Yield: 6 servings.

Raspberry Fluff

4 cups fresh raspberries	**1¹/₄ cups orange juice**
¹/₂ cup sugar	**¹/₄ cup lemon juice**

Place raspberries in a bowl and mash slightly. Sprinkle with ¹/₄ cup of sugar and let stand 30 minutes, stirring occasionally.

Combine orange juice and remaining ingredients in a small saucepan; cook over medium heat, stirring until sugar dissolves. Remove from heat, and let cool.

Place raspberry mixture in container of an electric blender or food processor; add juice mixture. Cover and process until smooth. Pour into an 8 inch square pan and freeze until almost firm. Spoon mixture into a large mixing bowl, and with an electric mixer, beat on medium speed until smooth. Return mixture to pan, and freeze until firm. Let stand at room temperature 10 minutes before serving. Yield: 8 servings.

Raspberry Yum-Yum from "The Lake"

2-3 cups ground up pretzels	**2 T. powdered sugar**
1 cup margarine, melted	

Combine and bake in a 9 x 12 inch pan in a 300° oven for 20 minutes. Cool.

1 (8 oz.) pkg. cream cheese	**³/₄ cup powdered sugar**
1 (8 oz.) carton cool whip	**1 egg**

Combine and spread over the cooled crust. Let set until firm.

1 (6 oz.) pkg. raspberry Jello	**2 pkgs. frozen raspberries**
2 cups boiling water	

Combine and let cool to room temperature. Pour over the above and refrigerate until firm. Yield: 1 dozen 3" squares.

Rhubarb Delight

1 cup flour	¹/₂ cup butter
5 T. powdered sugar	

Combine and pat in 8 " square pan. Bake 15 minutes in 350° oven.

Topping:

2 beaten eggs	¹/₄ cup flour
1¹/₂ cups sugar	³/₄ t. salt

Combine topping ingredients and then add **2 cups fresh diced rhubarb**. Pour into pan and bake at 350° for 25 minutes. Yield: 8-10 servings.

Rice Pudding

¹/₂ cup raisins	¹/₄ cup granulated sugar
1 cup rice, parboiled,	1 t. vanilla
not instant	2 cups heavy cream
2 cups milk	2 egg yolks

Combine raisins, rice, milk, sugar, and vanilla in a 2 quart souffle dish. Cook in microwave oven uncovered on HIGH for 10 minutes. Stir and cook for 10 minutes longer. Remove from oven. Whisk together cream and egg yolks, and stir into rice mixture. Cook, uncovered, for 1 minute. Stir and cook for 1 minute longer.

Remove from oven and stir. Let sit for 5 minutes before serving. Yield: 4 servings.

Shortbread

1 cup butter	³/₄ cup sugar
¹/₂ t. salt	3 cups flour

Beat butter and sugar until fluffy. Add salt and flour. Knead with hands. Place dough in a buttered circle pan or a 7 x 11 inch pan. Cut into wedges. Bake 350° for 20-25 minutes. Yield: 2 dozen.

Strawberries Romanoff

1 **quart fresh strawberries**
$^1/_2$ **cup sugar**
1 **cup heavy cream**
4 **T. brandy**

Select one cup berries. Mash and add sugar.

Whip cream and add to mashed berries. Stir in brandy. Refrigerate mixture and whole berries until needed.

To serve, pour sauce over whole berries in individual bowls. Yield: 4-6 servings.

Vanilla Pudding

$1^3/_4$ **cups milk** $^1/_2$ **cup cold milk**
$^1/_3$ **cup sugar**   1 **t. vanilla**
3 **T. cornstarch**

Heat the $1^3/_4$ cups milk in top of a double broiler over boiling water until bubbles appear around edge of milk. Combine sugar and cornstarch in a small bowl; stir in the $^1/_2$ cup cold milk until smooth. Gradually stir mixture into the heated milk.

Cook over boiling water, stirring constantly, until mixture thickens. Cover; cook over simmering water 20 minutes, stirring occasionally.

Remove from heat; stir in vanilla. Pour into serving dish; place a piece of plastic wrap directly on surface of pudding to prevent skin from forming. Cool to room temperature; refrigerate until cold.

Chocolate Pudding: Increase sugar to $^1/_2$ cup; add $^1/_3$ cup unsweetened cocoa powder and $^1/_8$ t. ground cinnamon with the cornstarch. Yield: 4-6 servings.

Cakes

Amaretto Bundt Cake

Angel Food Cake

Angel Food Cake a la Mauney

Apple Cake

Apple Cake with Toffee Sauce

Carrot Cake

Chocolate Zucchini Cake

Classic Chocolate Cake

Classic White Cake

Creme de Menthe Cake

Dump Cake

Guava Cake

Guava Cheesecake

Nacadoches Cake

No Bake Cheesecake

Oatmeal Cake

Oatmeal Cookie Cake

Petite Cherry Cheesecake

Rich Pound Cake

Sherry Bundt Cake

Yum-Yum Cake

Amaretto Bundt Cake

1   (18 ¹/₂ oz.) box yellow cake mix
1   (³/₄ oz.) box dry instant vanilla pudding
4   eggs
¹/₂   cup vegetable oil
¹/₂   cup Amaretto Liqueur
¹/₂   cup water

Beat all ingredients for 5 minutes and pour into a greased 12 cup bundt pan. Bake 350° for 45 minutes.

Glaze:

In a 4-cup measure, melt ¹/₂ **cup margarine** in a microwave on HIGH 1 minute in the microwave oven. Add ¹/₂ **cup sugar**, ¹/₄ **cup Amaretto Liqueur**, ¹/₄ **cup water**. Bring to boil on HIGH for 2 minutes. Stir once. Before removing from bundt dish make slits in the cake. Pour the hot glaze over cake in dish and let it stand several hours. Turn the cake out onto a serving plate. Yield: 24 servings.

Angel Food Cake

1¹/₂   cups cake flour
1¹/₂   cups granulated sugar
1¹/₂   cups egg whites (10-12)
1¹/₄   t. cream of tartar
¹/₄   t. salt
¹/₄   t. almond extract
1   t. vanilla extract

Sift flour and ¹/₂ cup sugar together four times. Set aside. Beat egg whites until foamy. Add cream of tartar and salt. Beat until peaks form. Add remaining sugar to egg whites, about 2 Tablespoons at a time. Add almond and vanilla extracts.

Fold flour into egg whites, about ¹/₄ cup at a time. Fold in until no flour shows. Do not beat. Spoon into an ungreased angel food cake pan and bake at 350° for 40 minutes. Yield: 14-16 slices.

Angel Food Cake a la Mauney

Prepare **1 angel food cake** as directed on the box.

Slice off entire top of baked cake about 1" down and set aside. Make cuts down into cake 1" from outer edge and 1" from edge of hole, leaving substantial "wall" on each side. With a curved knife or spoon remove cake within cuts, being careful to leave a base of cake 1" thick. Place cake on serving plate.

In chilled bowl, beat **3 cups chilled whipping cream, 1¹/₂ cups powdered sugar, ³/₄ cup cocoa** and **¹/₄ t. salt** until stiff. Fold **¹/₃ cup toasted slivered almonds** into half the whip cream mixture and spoon into cake cavity. Press mixture firmly to avoid "holes" in cut slices. Replace the cake top.

Frost cake with remaining whip cream mixture. Sprinkle with **¹/₃ cup slivered almonds**. Chill 4 hours. Yield: 12-16 servings.

"To test if a cake is done, use a piece of uncooked spaghetti if you do not have tooth picks."

Apple Cake

4	cups raw apples, diced	1	t. salt
2	cups sugar	2	t. baking soda
³/₄	cup oil	1	t. cinnamon
2	t. vanilla	1	t. nutmeg
1	cup chopped nuts	2	eggs, beaten
2	cups flour		

Mix sugar and apples until sugar disappears. Add oil, vanilla, and nuts. Mix flour and dry ingredients. Blend into mixture. Stir in eggs and pour into a 9 x 13 inch greased pan. Bake one hour at 350°. Yield: 10-12 servings.

Apple Cake with Toffee Sauce

4 cups chopped apples	**¹/₂ cup oil**
2 cups sugar	**2 eggs**

Combine the above and add to the apple mixture:

2 cups flour	**2 t. cinnamon**
2 t. baking soda	**³/₄ t. salt**
1 t. baking powder	**1 cup nuts**

Pour into a greased and floured 9 x 13 inch pan. Bake for 45-50 minutes in a 350° oven.

Toffee Sauce:

1 egg, beaten	**¹/₄ cup butter or margarine**
1 cup brown sugar	**¹/₄ cup orange juice**
¹/₈ t. salt	**¹/₄ cup water**

Stir on low heat until thickened or use the double boiler. Serve warm. Doubles nicely. Rewarm in jar in boiling water. Serve over the apple cake. Yield: 10-12 servings.

Mother's Day Brunch

Summertime Iced Tea, page 20
Cantaloupe Delight, page 162
Karl's Oat Bran Muffins, page 59
Banana Nut Bread, page 49
Breakfast Casserole, page 51
Spinach Quiche, page 109
Five Cup Salad, page 71
Nancy's Lemon Bars, page 204

Carrot Cake

2	cups flour		1	t. salt
1¹/₂	t. cinnamon		1	cup salad oil
2	cups sugar		4	eggs
2	t. baking soda		3	cups grated carrots

Icing:

1	(8 oz.) pkg. cream cheese		1	cup chopped nuts
¹/₂	cup margarine		2	t. vanilla
1	lb. box confectioner's sugar			

Sift and mix dry ingredients. Add oil and stir well. Add eggs one at a time. Add carrots. Pour into two 8-inch greased and floured pans and bake at 350° for 35-40 minutes or pour into a 9 x 13 inch greased and floured pan and bake at 350° for 40-45 minutes. Yield: 10-12 servings.

Icing: Beat well. Add nuts. Spread onto a completely cooled cake.

Chocolate Zucchini Cake

Beat together:

¹/₂	cup butter		2	eggs
¹/₂	cup oil		2	cups grated zucchini
1³/₄	cups sugar			

Add:

2¹/₂	cups flour		1	t. vanilla
¹/₂	cup cocoa		¹/₂	cup buttermilk or
1	t. baking soda			(¹/₂ cup milk and
1	t. salt			¹/₂ T. vinegar — let sit)

Mix thoroughly. Put in greased and floured 9 x 13 inch pan. Over batter sprinkle:

³/₄ **cup chocolate chips**   ³/₄ **cup chopped nuts**

Bake at 325° for 45 minutes. Yield: 10-12 servings.

Classic Chocolate Cake

3 oz. unsweetened chocolate,
   coarsely chopped
1/3 cup water
2 large eggs
1/2 cup unsalted butter, softened
1¹/2 cups dark brown sugar
2 cups flour
1¹/2 t. baking powder
1/2 t. baking soda
1/4 t. salt
3/4 cup sour cream

Preheat oven to 350°. Butter two 9 inch round cake pans. Line the bottoms with parchment or wax paper.

Melt chocolate and water. Cool slightly. Whisk in eggs. In large bowl with electric mixer, beat butter and brown sugar at medium speed until light and fluffy. Add chocolate mixture.

In medium bowl, toss together flour, baking powder, baking soda, and salt. Beat half into the batter at low speed. Beat in sour cream. Beat in remaining dry ingredients.

Pour into pans. Bake at 350° for 35 minutes. Transfer pans to rack, cool for 5 minutes, invert cakes onto the rack, peel off parchment paper, and let cool completely. Yield: 10-12 servings.

"Coat dates and nuts with a little flour before adding to cake batter to prevent them from settling on the bottom."

Classic White Cake

2 cups all-purpose flour	³/₄ cup milk
2 t. baking powder	2 t. vanilla
¹/₄ t. salt	1¹/₂ sticks (12 T.) unsalted butter,
6 large egg whites,	softened
at room temperature	1¹/₂ cups sugar

Preheat oven to 350°. Butter two 9" round cake pans. Line the bottoms with parchment or wax paper.

In medium bowl, stir together flour, baking powder, and salt. In another bowl beat egg whites, milk, and vanilla just to combine.

In a large bowl using an electric mixer, beat the butter and sugar with medium speed until light and fluffy.

At low speed beat dry ingredients alternately with egg mixture in 4 parts beginning and ending with dry ingredients. Stop to scrape bowl and beaters with rubber spatula after each addition.

Pour batter into pans. Bake at 350° for 25-30 minutes. Transfer pans to rack to cool for 5 minutes, then invert cakes onto the rack, peel off parchment paper, and let cool completely. Yield: 10-12 servings.

Creme de Menthe Cake

1 white cake mix	4 T. creme de menthe (divided)
2 egg whites	1 (16 oz.) can fudge frosting
1 cup plus 3 T. water	1 (8 oz.) Cool Whip, thawed

Beat together the first three ingredients for 2 minutes. Add 2 T. creme de menthe. Beat for one minute on low speed.

Pour into a greased 9 x 13 inch pan and bake at 350° for 25 minutes. Cool in pan. Top with fudge frosting. Mix together the Cool Whip and 2 T. creme de menthe and spread mixture on top of frosting. Yield: 10-12 servings.

Dump Cake

1	can cherry pie filling	½	cup chopped walnuts
1	large can crushed pineapple	½	cup butter
1	box yellow or white cake mix		

DUMP cherry pie filling and pineapple into a 9 x 13 inch glass pan.
Sprinkle cake mix over the fruit.
Sprinkle the walnuts on the top.
Slice the butter thinly over the top and bake at 350° for 1 hour. Yield: 10-12 servings.

Guava Cake

1	cup margarine	1½	t. baking soda
1½	cups sugar	½	t. each cinnamon,
4	eggs		cloves and salt
3	cups flour	1½	cups fresh sweetened
1	t. nutmeg		guava purée

Cream together the margarine and sugar. Add eggs, one at a time, beating well after each addition.

Sift together the dry ingredients and add to the egg mixture. Add the guava purée. Pour into two 9 inch greased layer pans and bake in the 350° for 30-35 minutes. Cool.

Frosting:

⅔	stick butter or margarine	⅓-½	cup guava purée
1	lb. box powdered sugar		

Cream butter with sugar and puree beating well until smooth and spreading consistency. Use as filling and frosting. Yield: 10-12 servings.

Guava Cheesecake

1¼   **cups graham cracker crumbs**

3   **T. sugar**

¼   **cup melted butter**

Combine and press mixture into bottom and sides of a 9 inch round spring pan and chill.

2   **(8 oz.) pkgs. cream cheese**

4   **eggs**

¾   **cup sugar**

1   **T. lemon juice**

½   **t. lemon rind**

In a large bowl, beat the cream cheese until smooth and add eggs, one at a time, beating well after each addition. Gradually add sugar, juice, and rind. Pour into prepared crust and bake in a 350° oven for 30 minutes.

Topping:

Blend **1 cup sour cream** with **2 T. sugar** and spread over warm cake. Return to oven for 10 minutes. Cool and refrigerate for 30 minutes.

Glaze:

Combine **1 T. cornstarch, ¼ cup water and ⅔ cup frozen guava concentrate** and cook over medium heat for 2-3 minutes, stirring constantly. Cool to room temperature; spread over cheesecake. Chill to serve. Yield: 10-12 servings.

"To prevent a soggy bottom cake: let the baked cake stand for five minutes in the cake pan and then unmold it onto a wire cake rack to permit air to circulate around the cake."

"For one cup cake flour: sift ⅞ cup all-purpose flour twice before measuring."

Nacadoches Cake

¹/₂	lb. margarine	2	cups sugar
¹/₂	cup Crisco	¹/₂	cup buttermilk
4	T. cocoa	2	eggs
1	cup water	1	t. baking soda
2	cups flour	1	t. vanilla

Frosting:

¹/₄	lb. margarine	1	cup walnuts
4	T. cocoa	¹/₂	t. vanilla
¹/₃	cup milk	1	lb. box powdered sugar

Bring to a boil first 4 ingredients, pour hot mixture over flour and sugar. Add buttermilk, eggs, baking soda, and vanilla. Pour into greased and floured 10 x 15 inch cookie sheet with sides. Bake 20 minutes at 400°. Five minutes before cake is done, mix and bring to boil margarine, cocoa, and milk. Remove from heat and add powdered sugar, nuts, and vanilla. Beat well. Spread on cake <u>immediately</u> upon removing from oven. Yield: 24 servings.

No Bake Cheesecake

1	(3 oz.) pkg. lemon Jello	1	can MILNOT (13 oz.), whipped
1	cup boiling water	3	cups graham cracker crumbs
1	(8 oz.) pkg. cream cheese	¹/₂	cup butter
1	cup sugar		or margarine, melted
3	T. lemon juice		

Dissolve gelatin in boiling water. Chill until slightly thickened. Cream together cheese, sugar, and lemon juice; add gelatin and blend well. Fold in stiffly whipped MILNOT. (Use electric mixer) Mix graham cracker crumbs and melted butter together; pack ²/₃ of mixture on bottom and sides of a 9 x 13 x 2 inch pan. Add filling and sprinkle with remaining crumbs. Chill several hours or overnight. Cut in squares and serve plain or garnish with fruit. Yield: 18-20 servings.

Oatmeal Cake

1¹/₂ cups boiling water	1¹/₂ cups flour
1 cup old-fashioned Quaker oats	2 eggs
1 cup sugar	1 t. baking soda
1 cup brown sugar	1¹/₂ t. cinnamon
¹/₂ cup margarine	¹/₂ t. salt

Topping:

1 cup brown sugar	¹/₃ cup evaporated milk
1 cup flaked coconut	

Mix oats with boiling water and let stand for 20 minutes. Mix all ingredients for the cake together and bake in a 9 x 12 inch greased pan at 350° for 30 minutes.

Mix all ingredients for topping and let stand while cake is baking. Immediately spread over top when cake is done and put under the broiler until it bubbles and is slightly brown. Yield: 10-12 servings.

Oatmeal Cookie Cake

1¹/₄ cups flour	2 eggs
¹/₂ t. baking soda	1 t. vanilla
¹/₂ t. salt	2¹/₂ cups uncooked
1 cup firmly packed	old fashioned oatmeal
brown sugar	¹/₂ cup chopped nuts
³/₄ cup butter or margarine	1 (6 oz.) pkg. mini-chocolate chips

Mix together flour, baking soda, salt and set aside. Mix the brown sugar and margarine together until fluffy. Blend in eggs and vanilla. Add dry ingredients and mix well. Stir in oatmeal, chips, and nuts. Spread over pizza pan (which has been sprayed with PAM) and bake for 17-20 minutes in a 350° oven. Yield: 10-12 servings.

Petite Cherry Cheesecake

 2   (8 oz.) pkgs. cream cheese, softened
³/₄ cup sugar
 2   eggs
 1   T. lemon juice
 1   t. vanilla
24   vanilla wafers
 1   (21 oz.) can cherry pie filling

Beat cream cheese, sugar, eggs, lemon juice, and vanilla until light and fluffy.
Line small muffin pans with paper bake cups, and place a vanilla wafer in bottom of
each cup. Fill the cups ²/₃ full with cream cheese mixture. Bake in 350° oven for 15-
20 minutes or until set. Top each with about 1 T. pie filling; chill. Yield: 2 dozen.

Rich Pound Cake

 1   pkg. Duncan Hines Supreme Cake Mix (lemon or orange)
 1   pkg. instant pudding (same flavor)
²/₃ cup Wesson oil
 4   eggs
 1   cup water (or orange juice)

Beat all ingredients together for 5 minutes.
Bake in greased tube pan in a 350° oven for 45 minutes. Yield: 24 servings.

Frosting:
For lemon or orange cake: blend ¹/₄ cup orange juice and ¹/₄ cup powdered sugar.
Drizzle over cake.

184

Sherry Bundt Cake

Cake:
- 1   pkg. yellow cake mix
- ³/₄   cup cream sherry
- 1   (3.4 oz.) pkg. instant vanilla pudding
- ³/₄   cup oil
- 4   eggs

Frosting:
- 1¹/₃   cups powdered sugar
- ¹/₂   cup cream sherry

Combine cake ingredients and beat with an electric mixer for 10 minutes. Pour into a 12 cup greased bundt cake pan. Bake 350° for 45 minutes. Pour frosting over top. Let set for a few hours before inverting onto cake plate. Yield: 24 servings.

Yum-Yum Cake

- 1   pkg. yellow cake mix
- 1   (8 oz.) pkg. cream cheese
- 1   (3.4 oz.) pkg. instant vanilla pudding
- 1   cup milk
- 1   (9 oz.) Cool Whip
- 1   (20 oz.) can crushed pineapple, drained
- 1¹/₂   cups coconut

Make cake according to mix directions. Bake in a greased 10 x 15 jelly roll pan. Cool 25 minutes. Cream the cream cheese. Mix instant pudding with 1 cup milk, add cream cheese to the pudding and mix until smooth. Add drained pineapple. Mix well. (If too thick to spread on cake add just a little pineapple juice). Spread pudding mixture on cooled cake. Put Cool Whip on top. Sprinkle coconut over Cool Whip.

Garnish with strawberry slices. Yield: 16-20 servings.

Pies

Apple Pie

Blueberry Pie

Blueberry-Banana Pie

Charleston Pecan Pie

Cherry Pie

Derby Pie

Farm Rhubarb Pie

Fresh Gooseberry Pie

Frozen Lemonade Pie

Fudge Nut Pie

Graham Cracker Crust

Key West Key Lime Pie

Mile-High Strawberry Pie

Mystery Pecan Pie

Nanny's Velvet Pie

Pumpkin Pie

Raspberry Dream Pie

Sour Cream Pie

Strawberry Pie

Washington State Berry Cobbler

Apple Pie

6-7	tart apples		dash of salt
¾	cup sugar		Pastry for 9 inch pie (2-crusts)
2	T. flour	2	T. butter
1	t. cinnamon		

Pare apples and slice thin. Combine sugar, flour, salt, and cinnamon. Mix with apples. Line the pie plate with pastry and fill with apple mixture; dot with butter. Adjust top crust. Bake in 400° oven for 50 minutes. Yield: 6-8 servings.

Blueberry Pie

4	cups blueberries	3	T. cornstarch
¾	cup sugar	¼	t. salt
¾	cup plus 2½ T. water	1	baked pie shell

Cook 1 cup of blueberries with sugar and ¾ cup water until berries are soft. Blend cornstarch, salt, and 2½ T. water. Stir into hot berries and cook slowly until thickened. Cool. Add 3 cups uncooked berries. Pour into cooled baked pie shell. Chill 3 hours. Yield: 8 servings.

Blueberry-Banana Pie

Crust makes 2—9" pies or 1—9 x 13" pan

1½	cups flour	½	cup chopped nuts
1½	sticks margarine	2	T. brown sugar

Combine and press into bottom of pans. Bake at 450° for about 10 minutes. Cool.
Filling:
Beat **2 envelopes Dream Whip** with **1 cup milk**. Add **8 oz. pkg. softened cream cheese, 1 cup sugar.** Beat till smooth. Slice **5 large bananas** onto bottom of cooled crust. Pour filling over and spoon **1 can blueberry pie filling** over the top. Refrigerate. Yield: 16-20 servings.

187

Charleston Pecan Pie

3	**eggs**
²/₃	**cup sugar**
1	**cup light corn syrup**
¹/₃	**cup melted margarine**
1	**cup pecan halves**
1	**9-inch unbaked pastry shell**

Beat eggs thoroughly with sugar, dash of salt, corn syrup, and margarine. Add pecans. Pour into unbaked pastry shell.

Bake in 350° oven for 50 minutes or until a knife inserted halfway between outside and center of filling comes out clean. Cool. Yield: 6-8 servings.

Cherry Pie

Make graham cracker crust in a 9" pie plate.

1¹/₂	**cups crushed graham crackers**
²/₃	**cup butter**
2	**T. sugar**

Bake at 350° for 8 minutes. Cool.

Cream together:

1	**(3 oz.) pkg. cream cheese, softened**
1	**pint whipping cream, whipped**
¹/₂	**cup sifted powdered sugar**
1	**t. vanilla**

Pour into crust and top with **Cherry pie filling** and **whipped cream**. Yield: 6-8 servings.

Derby Pie

1 cup sugar	¹/₂ cup flour
¹/₂ cup butter or margarine, melted	1 cup pecans, coarsely chopped
2 eggs, beaten	³/₄ cup chocolate chips
1 t. vanilla	1 9-inch unbaked pie shell

Stir sugar into melted and cooled butter. Add eggs, vanilla, and flour; blend well. Stir in pecans and chocolate chips. Pour into pie shell. Bake at 325° for 1 hour or until knife inserted halfway between center and edge comes out clean. Yield: 6-8 servings.

Farm Rhubarb Pie

3 cups raw rhubarb	2 T. flour
2 eggs	1 T. butter
¹/₂ cup sugar	¹/₂ t. nutmeg

Combine and put in an **unbaked pastry pie crust**. Bake in a 350° oven for 25 minutes. Yield: 6-8 servings.

Fresh Gooseberry Pie

3 cups fresh gooseberries	¹/₄ t. salt
1¹/₂ cups sugar	Pastry for 9 inch pie (2 crusts)
3 T. quick-cooking tapioca	2 T. butter

Crush ¹/₂ cup of gooseberries; combine with sugar, tapioca, and salt. Add the whole berries. Cook and stir until the mixture thickens. Line the pie plate with pastry. Put filling in unbaked pie crust and dot with butter and adjust top crust.

Bake in 450° oven for 10 minutes; reduce to 350° and bake about 30 minutes longer or until crust is done. Yield: 6-8 servings.

Frozen Lemonade Pie

1   (10 oz.) can sweetened condensed milk
1   (6 oz.) can frozen lemonade concentrate, thawed and undiluted
1   (8 oz.) container frozen whipped topping, thawed
2   9-inch prepared graham cracker crusts

Fold sweetened condensed milk and lemonade concentrate into whipped topping; spoon into crusts. Freeze until firm. Yield: 16 servings.

Fudge Nut Pie

¹/2   cup margarine
1   (6 oz.) semi-sweet chocolate
    morsels
¹/2   cup chopped pecans

¹/2   cup shredded coconut
1   cup sugar
2   eggs, beaten
1   baked 9 inch pastry shell

Microwave butter and morsels in a 2 quart glass dish on HIGH for 1 minute. Mix in sugar, pecans, coconut, then eggs. Pour filling into baked pastry shell. Microwave at 50% power for 8 minutes rotating dish ¹/4 turn at 2 minute intervals. Stir once after 4 minutes. Cool before serving. Yield: 6-8 servings.

Graham Cracker Crust

5   T. margarine (not butter)
1¹/4   cups graham crackers, crushed (or use gingersnaps)
1   T. sugar

Melt butter and add crushed graham crackers and sugar. Press firmly into a 9" pie pan. Bake in a 375° oven for 6-8 minutes or in a microwave oven on HIGH for 1¹/2-2 minutes. Cool before filling. Yield: 1 pie crust.

Key West Key Lime Pie

4   eggs, separated
1   can of sweetened condensed milk
3   oz. Key Lime juice

Beat the four egg yolks and one egg white until mixture is thick and lemon colored. Add condensed milk and beat again. Add lime juice, and beat until thick. Beat remaining 3 egg whites until stiff and dry, then fold into mixture.

Pour into a **graham cracker crust** (pg. 190) and bake in a 325° oven for 15 minutes. Chill. Before serving, top with **whipped cream**. Yield: 6-8 servings.

Mile-High Strawberry Pie

1   cup sugar
2   egg whites
1   (10 oz.) pkg. frozen strawberries, partially defrosted
1   t. vanilla
    dash of salt
1   T. lemon juice
1   cup cream, whipped
1   9 inch baked pastry or crumb pie shell

Mix sugar, egg whites, strawberries, vanilla, salt, and lemon juice in a large bowl. Beat at high speed until thick and fluffy at least until voluminous. Fold in whipped cream, and then pile into baked shell. Freeze for several hours. After pie is frozen, slice and serve frozen. Wrapped well in foil or plastic wrap, leftovers should keep at least two weeks. Yield: 6-8 servings.

Mystery Pecan Pie

1   **9 inch unbaked pastry shell**
1   **(8 oz.) pkg. cream cheese, softened**
¹/₃   **cup sugar**
¹/₄   **t. salt**
1   **t. vanilla**
1   **egg**
1¹/₄   **cups chopped pecans**

Topping:
¹/₄   **cup sugar**
1   **cup light corn syrup**
1   **t. vanilla**
3   **eggs**

Heat oven to 375°. In small bowl, combine cream cheese, sugar, salt, vanilla, and egg; blend until smooth. Spread in bottom of unbaked pastry shell. Sprinkle with pecans. In small bowl, combine topping ingredients; blend well. Pour over pecans. Bake 35 to 40 minutes until center is firm to touch. Cool before serving. Cut small pieces as this is very rich. Yield: 6-8 servings.

Nanny's Velvet Pie

1   **(3 oz.) pkg. lime, strawberry, or raspberry Jello**
¹/₄   **cup lemon juice**
¹/₄   **cup sugar**
1   **can condensed milk**

Mix Jello with ¹/₂ cup boiling water. Add lemon juice, sugar, and let cool. Pour one cold can condensed milk into large bowl and whip fast speed for at least 3 minutes. Then pour slowly into Jello mix. When done pour into a graham cracker pie shell. Save out ¹/₄ cup crumbs to add to top of pie for finishing touch. NO COOKING. Yield: 6-8 servings.

Pumpkin Pie

1½   **cups mashed, cooked pumpkin or canned pumpkin**
¾   **cup sugar**
½   **t. salt**
1   **t. cinnamon**
1   **t. ginger**
¼   **t. nutmeg**
½   **t. cloves**
3   **slightly beaten eggs**
1¼   **cups milk**
1   **(6 oz.) can evaporated milk**
1   **9-inch unbaked pastry shell**

Thoroughly combine the pumpkin, sugar, salt, and spices. Blend in eggs, milk, and pour into unbaked pastry shell. Bake in 400° oven for 50 minutes or until knife inserted halfway between center and outside comes out clean. Cool. Yield: 6-8 servings.

Raspberry Dream Pie

2   **egg whites**
   Dash of salt
¾   **cup sugar**
1   **(10 oz.) pkg. frozen raspberries, partially thawed and drained**
1   **T. lemon juice**
½   **cup whipping cream, whipped**
1   **t. vanilla**

Beat egg whites and salt until frothy. Add sugar slowly and beat until well mixed. Add raspberries, lemon juice and beat on HIGH for 10-15 minutes. This will become thick. Fold in whipping cream and vanilla. Pour mixture into baked, cooled 9 inch pie shell. Freeze at least 4 hours. Yield: 6-8 servings.

Sour Cream Pie

1	**9-inch unbaked pastry shell**
1	**cup sugar**
$^1/_2$	**t. cloves**
$^1/_2$	**t. cinnamon**
$^1/_4$	**t. salt**
2	**eggs, beaten**
2	**T. vinegar**
1	**cup raisins**
1	**cup sour cream**

Mix ingredients together stirring until sugar dissolves. Pour into pie shell; bake at 450° for 15 minutes; reduce heat to 350° and bake 25-30 minutes longer or until top is golden brown. Yield: 6-8 servings.

Strawberry Pie

Crust:

$^1/_2$	**cup butter**	$^1/_4$	**cup brown sugar**
1	**cup sifted flour**	$^1/_2$	**cup chopped pecans**

Make crust first by spreading into an oblong pan and bake for 15 minutes at 400°. Take from oven and press mixture against pan.

Filling: Line crust with **1 pint whole fresh strawberries**. Sprinkle lightly with **powdered sugar**. Cook **2 cups sliced berries** with **1 cup sugar** and **3 T. cornstarch** for 20 minutes. Add **2 T. lemon juice** and cook longer. Cool. Pour over whole berries to fill pie shell. Cool until ready to serve. Yield: 8-10 servings.

Washington State Berry Cobbler

4-6 **cups berries (wild blackberries, loganberries, boysenberries)**
³/₄ **cup sugar**
3 **T. margarine**
¹/₄ **t. salt**
1 **t. baking powder**
1 **cup flour**
¹/₂ **cup milk**

Put fruit in a 9 x 13 inch baking dish. Mix sugar, salt, flour, baking powder, and margarine together (as for pie crust). Add milk. Pour batter over fruit.

Mix together **1 cup sugar**, **2 T. cornstarch** and a pinch of **salt**. Sprinkle over dough; then pour **1 cup boiling water** over all and bake in 350° oven for one hour.

Serve with whipped cream or ice cream. Yield: 8-10 servings.

"For flaky pie crust, use bacon lard rather than shortening or butter."

"To prevent pie crust from getting soggy, brush with well beaten egg white."

"Reduce your oven by 25° when baking with glass containers."

"Beaten egg whites if not used immediately will become watery and the air will have escaped."

Cookies

Blondies - Brownies

Boulder Chocolate Chip Cookies

Brownies - Microwave

Caramel Filled Chocolate Cookies

Carrot and Zucchini Bars

Chocolate Frosting for Brownies

Chocolate Squares

Congo Squares

Ginger Snaps • Lace Cookies

Macaroons

Macadamia-Coconut Bars

Madeira Cookies • Mint Brownies

Molasses Sugar Cookies

Nancy's Lemon Bars

Nelson Medical Group Brownies

Peanut Butter Bars

Peanut Butter Cookies

Pecan Tassies • Sherry Bars

Super Simple Peanut Butter Cookies

Swedish Spritz

Waffle Stomper Cookies

Blondies — Brownies

³/₄	cup butter, softened	2	cups flour
³/₄	sugar	2	t. baking powder
³/₄	cup dark brown sugar	1	cup milk chocolate chips
3	eggs	3-4	oz. white chocolate bar, chopped
1	t. vanilla		

Cream butter and sugars together. Add eggs, flour, baking powder, and vanilla. Mix well. Add chocolates and pour into a well greased 9 x 13 inch pan and bake in a 350° oven for 30-35 minutes. Yield: 2 dozen.

Boulder Chocolate Chip Cookies

1	cup soft butter	1	t. baking soda
1	cup brown sugar	1	t. salt
1	cup sugar	2	cups flour
2	eggs	2¹/₂	cups regular oatmeal crushed with rolling pin in a zip-top bag
1	t. vanilla		
1	t. baking powder	¹/₂	cup chocolate chips

Cream butter, brown sugar, and white sugar together. Add eggs and vanilla. Add baking powder, baking soda, and salt to flour and stir into the egg and sugar mixture. Stir in crushed oatmeal and chocolate chips. Place by tablespoons on an ungreased cookie sheet and bake in a 350° oven for 10-12 minutes. Yield: 4 dozen.

Brownies — Microwave

2 (1 oz. each) squares unsweetened chocolate	$^1/_2$ t. vanilla
	$^3/_4$ cup all-purpose flour
$^1/_3$ cup butter or margarine	$^1/_2$ t. baking powder
1 cup sugar	$^1/_2$ t. salt
2 eggs	$^1/_2$ cup nuts, chopped

Place chocolate and butter in a 4-cup measuring cup and melt in a microwave on 50% power for $2^1/_2$ minutes or until mixture is melted. Stir 2-3 times during melting.

Stir in sugar, eggs, and vanilla. Beat well. Combine flour, baking powder, and salt. Blend well. Stir into chocolate mixture. Stir in nuts. Spread evenly in a greased 8 x 8 x 2 inch dish or an 8 inch round dish.

Bake in microwave oven full power for $4^1/_2$ minutes or until top springs back when lightly pressed with finger. Cool. Cut into squares. Yield: 16 2" squares.

Caramel Filled Chocolate Cookies

1 cup butter or margarine	1 t. baking soda
1 cup sugar	2 t. vanilla
1 cup firmly packed light brown sugar	1 cup chopped pecans, divided in half
2 eggs	1 T. sugar
$2^1/_4$ cups all purpose flour	1 (9 oz.) pkg chewy caramels in chocolate (ROLOS)
$^3/_4$ cup cocoa	

Beat butter at medium speed until creamy. Gradually add sugars, beating well. Add eggs. Beat well. Add flour, cocoa, and baking soda. Stir in vanilla and $^1/_2$ cup chopped pecans. Cover cookie dough and refrigerate for one hour. Combine remaining $^1/_2$ cup pecans and 1 T. sugar. Set aside. Gently press 1 T. cookie dough around each candy, forming a ball. Dip one side of cookie in pecan mixture. Place pecan side up, 2 inches apart on ungreased cookie sheet. Bake in a 375° oven for 8 minutes. Cookies will look soft; let cool 1 minute on cookie sheets, remove to wire racks to cool. Yield: 4 dozen.

Carrot and Zucchini Bars

¹/₂	cup flour	1	medium zucchini,
³/₄	cup packed brown sugar		shredded (1 cup)
1	t. baking powder	¹/₂	cup raisins
¹/₂	t. ground ginger	¹/₂	cup chopped walnuts
¹/₄	t. baking soda	¹/₂	cup oil
2	eggs, slightly beaten	¹/₄	cup honey
¹/₂	cup shredded carrot	1	t. vanilla

In a mixing bowl, stir together the flour, brown sugar, baking powder, ginger, and baking soda. Set aside.

In a medium mixing bowl, stir together the eggs, carrot, zucchini, raisins, walnuts, oil, honey, and vanilla. Add the carrot mixture to flour mixture. Using a wooden spoon, stir just until combined.

Spread the batter into an ungreased 13 x 9 x 2 inch baking pan. Bake in a 350° oven about 25 minutes or until a wooden toothpick inserted near the center comes out clean. Cool in pan on a wire rack. Spread with orange-cream cheese frosting over cooled bars. Store, covered, in refrigerator. Yield: 3 dozen.

Orange-Cream Cheese Frosting:

In small mixing bowl, combine **one (8 oz.) package light cream cheese, ¹/₂ cup sifted powdered sugar, 2 T. orange juice,** and **1 T. finely shredded lemon peel or orange peel**. Beat with an electric mixer until light and fluffy.

Chocolate Frosting for Brownies

2	T. butter	1	t. vanilla
1	square unsweetened chocolate	2	cups powdered sugar
2	T. warm water or milk		

Melt butter and chocolate over low heat. Stir in water or milk and vanilla. Remove from heat and stir in powdered sugar. Blend well. Frost cooled Microwave Brownies (page 198) or Waffle Stomper Cookies (page 208).

Chocolate Squares

Crust:

2 cups flour	1 cup butter
½ cup nuts	2 T. sugar

Cream butter, flour, nuts, and sugar. Spread over 9 x 13 inch pan. Bake 15 minutes at 400° or until light brown.

Filling:

1 (8 oz.) pkg. cream cheese	1 (13 ½ oz.) Cool Whip (use half)
¾ cup powdered sugar	

Cream cheese and sugar. Add Cool Whip, mix, spread over cooled crust.

Pudding:

2 (3.4 oz.) pkgs. instant chocolate pudding	3 cups milk

Beat together. Pour over filling mixture. Place rest of Cool Whip on top. Shave bits of chocolate and sprinkle on top if desired. Chill.

Note: you may substitute lemon pudding for the chocolate to make lemon squares. Yield: 2 dozen.

Congo Squares

2¾ cups flour	3 eggs
2½ t. baking powder	1 t. vanillla
½ t. salt	1 (6 oz.) pkg. semi-sweet chocolate pieces
⅔ cup shortening or butter	
1 box brown sugar	½ cup walnuts, finely chopped

Combine flour, baking powder, salt, soft butter, and brown sugar. Mix well. Add eggs, one a time, beating after each. Add vanilla, nuts, and chocolate.

Bake at 350° for 25-30 minutes in 10 x 15 x ⅜" pan. Cut into squares. Yield: 3 dozen.

Mint Brownies

First Layer:

- $^1/_2$ cup butter
- 2 oz. unsweetened chocolate
- 2 eggs
- 1 cup sugar
- $^1/_2$ cup plus 2 T. sifted flour
- $^1/_8$ t. salt
- 1 t. vanilla
- $^1/_2$ cup chopped nuts

Second Layer:

- $1^1/_2$ cups sifted powdered sugar
- 3 T. butter
- 2 T. milk
- 1 t. peppermint extract
  green food coloring

Chocolate Glaze:

- 3 oz. semi-sweet chocolate
- 3 T. butter

Melt butter and chocolate together. Beat eggs and sugar until ivory color. Add flour, salt, vanilla, nuts, and chocolate mixture. Pour into greased and floured 9 inch square pan. Bake at 350° for 25 minutes.

For second layer, beat together all the ingredients and several drops of green food coloring. Spread mint cream over baked bottom. Chill until firm.

Prepare chocolate glaze by melting chocolate and butter together. Pour over chilled mint cream and chill again until firm. Cut into squares. Yield: 16 squares. Double recipe may be made in a 9 x 13 inch pan.

Molasses Sugar Cookies

$^3/_4$ cup shortening	$^1/_4$ t. salt
1 cup sugar	$^1/_2$ t. cinnamon
1 egg	$^1/_2$ t. ginger
$^1/_4$ cup molasses	$^1/_2$ t. cloves
2 cups all-purpose flour	sugar
2 t. baking soda	

Cream shortening; gradually add 1 cup sugar, beating at medium speed of electric mixer until light and fluffy. Add egg and molasses; mix well.

Combine flour, soda, salt, and spices; mix well. Add about $^1/_4$ of dry mixture at a time to creamed mixture, mixing until smooth after each addition. Chill dough at least 1 hour.

Shape dough into 1 inch balls and roll in sugar. Place 2 inches apart on ungreased cookie sheets. Bake at 375° for 10 minutes. Cool on wire racks. Yield: 4 $^1/_2$ dozen.

For Gingersnaps: Prepare Molasses Sugar Cookies, omitting cloves, and increasing ground ginger to 1 Tablespoon.

Nancy's Lemon Bars

2 cups sifted flour	1 cup butter
$^1/_2$ cup powdered sugar	

Cut in with a pastry blender and pat into 9 x 13 x 2 inch pan and bake for 20-25 minutes in a 350° oven.

4 eggs, beaten	$^1/_4$ cup flour
2 cups sugar	$^1/_2$ t. baking powder
$^1/_3$ cup lemon juice	

Mix and bake over the first layer for 25 minutes in a 350° oven. Yield: 2 dozen.

Nelson Medical Group Brownies

4 cups graham cracker crumbs	1 (12 oz.) pkg. chocolate chips
1 cup nuts	1 cup evaporated milk
1/2 cup sifted powdered sugar	1 t. vanilla

Mix graham cracker crumbs, nuts, and sugar together. Set aside. Melt chocolate chips and milk on low heat stirring constantly. Add vanilla.

Set aside 1/2 cup of the chocolate mixture and stir the rest into the crumb mixture. Press into 9 x 9 inch buttered dish and pour the 1/2 cup chocolate mixture over. Chill before cutting. Yield: 3 dozen.

Peanut Butter Bars

1 cup butter or margarine	2 cups graham cracker crumbs
1 cup peanut butter	1 (12 oz.) pkg. chocolate chips
1 lb. powdered sugar	

Melt butter, add peanut butter, sugar, and cracker crumbs. Mix together and pat into 9 x 13 inch pan. Melt chocolate chips and spread on top. Refrigerate for a little while to firm. Yield: 2 dozen.

Peanut Butter Cookies

1 cup sugar	1 cup real peanut butter
1 cup brown sugar	3 cups all-purpose flour
1 cup shortening	2 t. baking soda
2 eggs	1/2 t. salt
1 t. vanilla	

Cream sugars, shortening, eggs, and vanilla. Stir in peanut butter. Add dry ingredients. Drop by rounded teaspoons on ungreased cookie sheet. Press with back of floured fork to make indentation. Bake in 350° oven for about 10 minutes. Yield: 5 dozen.

Pecan Tassies

1 (3 oz.) pkg. cream cheese	1 cup flour
¹/₂ cup margarine or butter	

Cream butter and cheese; stir in flour. Chill about 1 hour. Then shape into 36 balls. The balls should be about ¹/₂ inch in diameter. Place in ungreased 1 inch muffin cups and press against bottom and sides with a flat-bottomed shot glass dipped in flour — or just use your fingers. Fill with pecan filling. Yield: 3 dozen.

Pecan Filling:

1 egg	1 t. vanilla
³/₄ cup brown sugar	Dash of salt
1 T. butter	²/₃ cup pecans, chopped

Beat egg, sugar, butter, vanilla, and salt until smooth. Add nuts. Fill muffin cups with mixture. Bake at 325° for 25 minutes or until set. Cool and remove from pans. Recipe can be doubled and tripled easily.

Bridal Shower Luncheon Buffet

Sherry Bars

4 oz. unsweetened chocolate	$^1/_2$ t. salt
1 cup butter	1 cup flour
4 eggs	1 t. vanilla
2 cups sugar	

Preheat oven 325°. Melt chocolate and butter. Cool. Beat eggs. Add sugar, salt and cooled chocolate mixture. Stir in vanilla and flour. Pour into a greased and floured 9 x 13 inch baking pan. Bake 30-40 minutes. Cool.

Beat the following ingredients and spread over the cooked chocolate layer. Then chill.

$^1/_2$ cup butter, melted	1 cup chopped pecans
1 lb. powdered sugar	$^1/_4$ cup pale dry sherry
$^1/_4$ cup heavy cream (beat until stiff)	

Combine and heat the following ingredients to melt. Spread over chilled layers. Chill, or serve at room temperature. Yield: 2 dozen.

6 oz. semi-sweet chocolate chips	3 T. water
4 T. butter	

Super Simple Peanut Butter Cookies

1 cup peanut butter
1 egg
1 cup sugar

Beat together. Form 1 inch balls and press onto an ungreased cookie sheet with a fork. Bake 350° degrees for 10 minutes. (This recipe calls for NO flour, baking soda, or baking powder.) Yield: 2 dozen.

Swedish Spritz

1¹/₂	cups butter	1	t. almond extract
1	cup sugar	4	cups all-purpose flour
1	egg	1	t. baking powder
1	t. vanilla		

Cream first 5 ingredients. Add a few drops of food coloring if you desire colored cookies. Add dry ingredients. Mix until smooth. Do not chill.

Force dough through cookie press, forming various shapes, on ungreased cookie sheet. Bake in 400° oven about 8-10 minutes. Remove from sheets and cool. Yield: 6 dozen.

Waffle Stomper Cookies

2	(1 oz. each) squares unsweetened chocolate	³/₄	cup sugar
		1	cup flour
¹/₄	cup margarine	1	t. vanilla
2	eggs	¹/₂	t. salt

Frosting:

2	cups powdered sugar	¹/₄	cup margarine
¹/₄	cup cocoa	2-3	T. milk

Melt chocolate and butter. Remove from heat. Beat eggs and stir in sugar. Add chocolate to mixture. Fold in flour, salt, and vanilla. Drop by teaspoons on heated waffle iron. Close iron and bake 90 seconds. Cool on rack. Combine frosting ingredients and spread on top. Yield: 3 dozen.

Candy

Buckeyes

Cherry Chocolate Candy

Dinner Mint Fudge

English Toffee

Magic Shell

Microwave Rocky Road Candy

Peanut Butter Fudge

See's Fudge

Toffee

Two Minute Fudge

Buckeyes

1 lb. margarine at room temperature
3 lb. powdered sugar
2 lb. peanut butter
3 T. vanilla

Cream butter, add sugar, and blend. Add peanut butter and vanilla, mixing with hands until smooth. Roll into small balls and put on waxed paper or cookie sheet and refrigerate for 2 hours.

One-half hour before removing, melt the chocolate covering:

In a double broiler slowly melt:

2 (12 oz.) pkgs. semi-sweet chocolate pieces
2 (1 oz.) squares unsweetened chocolate
$^1/_2$ block paraffin

Take cookie sheets out of the refrigerator one at a time. Toothpick ball and dip into chocolate leaving center clear.

Place back on waxed paper sheet. Keep in cool place in an air-tight container.

Do not refrigerate. Keeps for weeks. Yield: 8 dozen.

"Never beat egg whites in a plastic bowl. Plastic retains traces of grease. Best to use a copper, glass, or metal bowl."

"To test for egg freshness, put the egg in a bowl of cold water. If it sinks, it is fresh. If fairly fresh, it will bob up on one end. If stale, it will float."

Cherry Chocolate Candy

2 cups sugar	1 t. vanilla
²/₃ cup evaporated milk	10 oz. salted peanuts
dash of salt	³/₄ cup peanut butter
12 large marshmallows	1 T. margarine
½ cup margarine	1 (12 oz.) pkg. chocolate chips
1 (6 oz.) pkg. cherry baking chips	

Combine sugar, milk, salt, marshmallows, and ½ cup margarine in saucepan over medium heat. Boil 5 minutes. Remove from heat. Add cherry chips and vanilla. Pour into 9 x 13 inch buttered pan. Melt chocolate chips in double boiler. Add peanut butter, 1 T. margarine, and crushed, salted peanuts. Spread over cherry mixture and chill. Yield: 2 dozen.

Dinner Mint Fudge

2 cups sugar	2 T. light corn syrup
¹/₃ cup cocoa	¹/₄ cup butter or margarine
pinch of salt	3 T. creme de menthe
²/₃ cup milk	

Combine first 5 ingredients in a heavy 3 quart saucepan; cook over medium heat, stirring constantly, until mixture boils. Cover and boil 3 minutes. Remove cover, and cook until mixture reaches soft ball stage (234°). Remove from heat; cool 10 minutes. Add butter and creme de menthe; beat until slightly thickened about 2 minutes. Pour mixture into a buttered 8 inch square pan. Cool and cut into 2 inch squares. Yield: 16 squares.

English Toffee

1   **lb. butter (do not substitute)**
2   **heaping cups sugar**
1   **(12 oz.) pkg. semi-sweet chocolate chips**
8   **oz. milk chocolate bar or chips**
2   **cups chopped pecans**

Place butter and sugar in large (4 qt.) pan. Place on medium heat, stir constantly. Boil until a glossy bronze color (hard crack stage). Add pecans and mix. Pour into cookie sheet and let cool. Remove from sheet and place on wax paper. Melt 6 oz. semi-sweet and 4 oz. milk chocolate and spread evenly over toffee. Do same to other side.

Magic Shell

$^1/_2$ **lb. butter**
1   **(12 oz.) pkg. semi-sweet chocolate pieces**
1   **cup coarsely chopped walnuts or pecans**

In double broiler, melt butter and chocolate pieces, stirring until mixture is smooth. Stir in nuts. Serve hot over very cold ice cream. Sauce will harden when it comes in contact with the ice cream. Refrigerate left-overs and reheat before using. Yield: 2 cups.

Microwave Rocky Road Candy

1   **(12 oz.) pkg. chocolate chips**   2   **cups cocktail peanuts**
1   **(6 oz.) pkg. butterscotch chips** $1^3/_4$ **cups miniature**
1   **cup peanut butter**   **marshmallows**

Layer chocolate and butterscotch chips and peanut butter in a glass casserole. Microwave on HIGH for 3 minutes or until easily mixed; add nuts and marshmallows. Pour into greased 9 x 11 inch glass dish. Refrigerate. Hardens in a heartbeat.

Peanut Butter Fudge

Boil for 5 minutes:

- 1 **cup sugar**
- 1 **cup brown sugar**
- $^1/_2$ **cup evaporated milk**
- **dash of salt**

Stir in:

- 1 **cup marshmallow cream**
- $^3/_4$ **cup smooth or crunchy peanut butter**
- 1 **T. butter**
- 1 **t. vanilla**

Pour into a buttered 9 x 9 inch pan. Yield: 3 dozen.

See's Fudge

- $^1/_2$ **cup plus 2 T. butter**
- 2 **t. vanilla**
- 1$^1/_2$ **cups chocolate chips**
- 10 **large marshmallows, cut up**
  or 80 small marshmallows
- $^3/_4$ **cup plus 2 T. evaporated milk**
- 1 **cup chopped nuts**

Place 6 T. butter, vanilla, and chocolate chips in a large electric mixer bowl; set aside.

Melt remaining butter and marshmallows in a double boiler. In another pan bring sugar and evaporated milk to a rolling boil, to soft ball stage. Pour butter and melted marshmallows over ingredients in bowl. Add boiling sugar and milk. Beat vigorously until creamy or 5 minutes with electric beater. Add chopped nuts and pour into 8 x 8 inch pan, buttered. Candy sets quickly. Yield: 16 pieces.

Toffee

   1   **cup butter**
1 $^1/_3$ **cups sugar**
   1   **T. corn syrup**
   2   **T. water**

Blend the ingredients together and microwave in a 2 quart glass measuring cup on HIGH for 4 minutes.

Stir. Cook again on HIGH for 6-8 minutes or to 300°. Stir in **1 t. vanilla** and $^1/_3$ **cup nuts**, chopped.

Pour into buttered cookie sheet and score with knife or pastry wheel.

Top with:

   $^1/_2$ **cup chocolate pieces, melted**
   $^1/_4$ **cup nuts, finely chopped**

Chill and break into pieces.

Two Minute Fudge

   1   **box confectioners' sugar**
   $^1/_2$ **cup cocoa**
   $^1/_2$ **cup butter, cut in quarters**
   1   **T. vanilla**
   $^1/_2$ **cup chopped nuts**
   $^1/_4$ **cup milk**

Place sugar, cocoa, butter, and milk in a large mixing bowl. Microwave on HIGH for 2 minutes.

Remove from oven, stir well, mixing in vanilla. When fudge loses its gloss, add nuts and pour into a buttered dish.

Chill 20-30 minutes. Cut into squares.

Miscellaneous

Miscellaneous
Breadcrumbs
Mango Chutney
Mayonnaise
Microwave Croutons

USS Tillman (DD641). Bow Assembly in vertical position prior to moving into position for fitting to the forward section. 28 October 1941.

Breadcrumbs

1 lb. white bread

Trim crust from bread. Crumble bread in food processor.
Spread crumbs in a thin layer in a 13 x 9 oval dish. Cook, uncovered in a microwave oven on HIGH for 8 minutes, stirring twice during cooking. Remove from oven. Cool. Store tightly covered. Can reprocess for finer breadcrumbs. Yield: 2 cups.

Mango Chutney

3 cups sugar	**¹/₄ cup chopped crystallized ginger**
1 cup white vinegar	**1 garlic clove, crushed**
6 cups sliced mangoes, peeled	**1 t. salt**
1 cup sliced onions	**¹/₂ t. mustard seed**
¹/₂ cup raisins	**1 chili pepper, crushed**

Combine sugar and vinegar in large pan. Stir over high heat until boiling. Add remaining ingredients and cook over medium heat until slightly thickened (about one hour). Stir occasionally to prevent burning. Pour into hot sterilized jars. Seal. Yield: 7 (¹/₂ pint) jars.

Mayonnaise

1 large whole egg	**dash of cayenne**
¹/₂ t. salt, or salt to taste	**2 T. lemon juice or vinegar**
¹/₄ t. paprika	**1 cup salad oil**
dash of white pepper	

In blender combine egg and seasonings. Beat in 1 T. of the lemon juice or vinegar. Gradually add in oil on low speed. Add the other 1 T. lemon juice or vinegar. Store in refrigerator. Yield: 1 cup.

Microwave Croutons

4 cups cubed bread
1 T. garlic herb seasoning

Combine in 12 x 8 baking dish. Toss well. Microwave on HIGH for 6-8 minutes stirring every 2 minutes. Cool thoroughly and store in air-tight container. Yield: 4 cups.

On 28 August, 1961, the Marshlands Plantation house was moved to make room for the new dry dock. Resting on two barges, it is moved through Charleston Harbor to Fort Johnson.

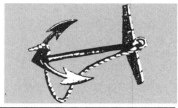

USS Tunny (SSN-682)

228

DONNA L. KAUP

Donna L. Kaup is a native of Seattle, Washington. As a registered nurse she has worked at the University of Washington Hospital in Seattle, WA; medical clinics in San Diego, CA; New London, CT; Charleston, SC; and as a campus nurse at Madeira School for Girls in McLean, VA.

She has been a navy wife for over 25 years. Thirteen times she has moved with her husband, Karl, and their three daughters Stacy, Jennifer, and Amy to various submarine ports: Bremerton, WA; San Diego, CA; New London, CT; Pearl Harbor, HI; and Charleston, SC. Three tours of duty were spent in Washington, DC. Taking advantage of her husband's submarine deployments, she traveled to meet him in Hong Kong, Yokosuka, Subic Bay, London, and Sardinia.

Besides traveling, her other interests include sewing, knitting, cooking, quilting, scuba diving, aviation, and skiing.

Actively involved in wives clubs across the nation, she has been instrumental in the creation of three other cookbooks: <u>Dolphin Delicacies</u> (Pearl Harbor Submarine Wives); <u>The Force's Finest</u> (Submarine Officers' Wives' Club of Charleston); and <u>Salad Celebration</u> (Naval Officers' Wives' Club of San Diego).

Donna and her husband lived at Quarters A on the Charleston Naval Base from November 1991 to October 1993.

PHOTO CREDITS

Gateway Publications, Inc.
P. O. Box 873,
Charleston, SC 29402
Phone: 803-722-3969 • Fax: 803-853-6901

Please send _____ copy (copies)   @ $16.95 each_____
   Postage and handling   @ $ 3.00 each_____
   South Carolina Residents add Sales Tax   @ $1.02 each_____
                                  Total_____

Name_____

Address_____

City _____ State _____ Zip_____

Make checks payable to Dining in Quarters A

==

Gateway Publications, Inc.
P. O. Box 873,
Charleston, SC 29402
Phone: 803-722-3969 • Fax: 803-853-6901

Please send _____ copy (copies)   @ $16.95 each_____
   Postage and handling   @ $ 3.00 each_____
   South Carolina Residents add Sales Tax   @ $1.02 each_____
                                  Total_____

Name_____

Address_____

City _____ State _____ Zip_____

Make checks payable to Dining in Quarters A

==

Gateway Publications, Inc.
P. O. Box 873,
Charleston, SC 29402
Phone: 803-722-3969 • Fax: 803-853-6901

Please send _____ copy (copies)   @ $16.95 each_____
   Postage and handling   @ $ 3.00 each_____
   South Carolina Residents add Sales Tax   @ $1.02 each_____
                                  Total_____

Name_____

Address_____

City _____ State _____ Zip_____

Make checks payable to Dining in Quarters A